DATE DUE

DISCARD

DEMCO 38-296

100

GREAT POEMS OF THE TWENTIETH CENTURY

Also by Mark Strand

Sleeping with One Eye Open (1964)

Reasons for Moving (1968)

Darker (1970)

The Story of Our Lives (1973)

The Late Hour (1978)

The Monument (1978)

Selected Poems (1980)

The Continuous Life (1990)

Dark Harbor (1993)

Blizzard of One: Poems (1998)

100
GREAT POEMS OF THE TWENTIETH CENTURY

Mark Strand

W. W. NORTON & COMPANY

NEW YORK LONDON

Since this page cannot legibly accommodate all the copyright notices, pages
305–315 constitute an extension of the copyright page.

Manufacturing by Courier Westford
Book design by Chris Welch Design
Production manager: Julia Druskin

Library of Congress Cataloging-in-Publication Data

100 great poems of the twentieth century / edited by Mark Strand.— 1st ed.
p. cm.
Includes index.
ISBN 0-393-05894-8 (hardcover)
1. Poetry—20th century—Translations into English. 2. English poetry—
20th century. 3. American poetry—20th century. I. Strand, Mark, 1934–
PN6101.A163 2005
821'.9108—dc22

2005002150

W. W. Norton & Company, Inc., 500 Fifth Avenue, New York, N.Y. 10110
www.wwnorton.com

W. W. Norton & Company Ltd., Castle House, 75/76 Wells Street, London W1T 3QT

1 2 3 4 5 6 7 8 9 0

For Andrew Zawacki,
who did so much to make this book a reality.

Contents

PREFACE

Every anthology is a personal one, reflecting the editor's taste and, it is hoped, his good judgment. I doubt if any two editors would come up with identical lists of one hundred great twentieth-century poems, nor would they have the same reasons for their choices. The truth is that there are many more than one hundred, surely more than enough to satisfy a variety of tastes. I have not chosen *the* hundred great poems, but *a* hundred great poems. They are poems that I have continued to feel strongly about over the years and that for one reason or another will not allow themselves to be forgotten or pushed aside by other more recent poems. They reflect the many changes—some cataclysmic, others gradual—that have been part of the literary history of the last century. Keeping the reader—the common reader—in mind, I have chosen poems that require no special knowledge for their appreciation and that can be read more than once without diminishing their power to persuade, amuse, or entrance. I have tried to include long poems as well as short ones, and experimental poems along with traditional ones. I have also tried to strike a balance between what might be the expected choices in such an anthology and what might be surprising ones.

The limitations of this book are of course my own limitations. The poets represented are from North and South America and Europe. Since I know very little of the literatures of Africa and Asia, I have not attempted to represent them. Were more translations available from the many languages of those two continents, I might have tried. By far the largest representation is from North America, especially the United States, which has produced an extraordinary number of gifted poets. In order to effect some balance in the anthology, I have kept the number of American poets to fewer than fifty. But the abundance and availability of American poems created a problem: how to select so few from so many? The solution was to select from a smaller pool. I decided not to choose work from anyone born after 1927. I did, however, make exceptions for several non-Americans: Dan Pagis, Thom Gunn, Derek Walcott, Tomas Tranströmer, and Inger Christensen.

I have said that the poems I chose reflect some of the changes in the literary history of the past century. It should be added that they reflect in various ways the century itself. But they are not glosses or histories. Their documentary value, if it exists at all, is slight. What one may discover in these poems are the identifying features of many individual imaginations that managed to be productive in what Elizabeth Bishop once called "our worst century so far." In vastly different ways, they provide us with what experiencing that century was like. Its wars, its social upheavals, its weathers, and its brief periods of calm, however illusory, will be present only to the degree that they involved each poet. It stands to reason that some poets will seem only slightly affected by public or political events while others will be consumed by them. What is most important, however, is how these individual responses have been shaped into what we recognize as poems. Tone and texture of feeling have at least as much to do with what a poem is about as any assessment of what its subject matter is. It has not been the purpose of this anthology to provide a coherent picture of the last century. With so many voices, each obeying its own logic and setting its own limits for what can and cannot be said, it would not have been possible, or desirable. Thus I have welcomed as many contrasting views and visions as my own editorial taste would allow. The result, I hope, is an anthology that is as lively as it is readable.

I was unable to attain permission from the Mistral estate to reprint Ursula Le Guin's beautiful translation of Gabriela Mistral's poem "La Huella" ("The Footprint"). Since this reversal of fortune came late in the book's production, the only available solution seemed to be the addition of a poem by a poet whose name was alphabetically close to Mistral's. Hence the decision to include a second poem by the great Polish poet Miłosz.

100

GREAT POEMS OF THE TWENTIETH CENTURY

ANNA AKHMATOVA

Translated from the Russian by Judith Hemschemeyer

Northern Elegies

Everything is a sacrifice to your memory . . .—PUSHKIN

FIRST
Prehistory

I no longer live there . . .—PUSHKIN

Dostoevsky's Russia. The moon,
Almost a quarter hidden by the bell tower.
Pubs are bustling, droshkies flying,
In Gorokhovaya, near Znameniya and Smolny,
Huge, five-storied monstrosities are growing.
Dance classes everywhere, money changers' signs,
A line of shops: "Henriette," "Basile," "André"
And magnificent coffins: "Shumilov Senior."
But still, the city hasn't changed much.
Not only I, but others as well,
Have noticed that sometimes it could
Resemble an old lithograph,
Not first class, but fairly decent,
From the Seventies, I'd guess.
       Especially in winter, before dawn,
       Or at twilight—then behind the gates
       Liteiny Boulevard darkens, rigid, straight,
       Not yet disgraced by the Moderne,
       And opposite me live—Nekrasov
       And Saltikov . . . Each on his memorial plaque.
       Oh, how horrified they would be
       To see those plaques! I move on.

And the splendid ditches of old Russa,
And the rotting arbors in the little gardens,

And a windowpane as black as a hole in the ice,
And it seems that such things happened here
That we'd better not look in. Let's leave.
Not every place agrees
To render up its secrets
(And I won't be in Optina anymore . . .)

The rustle of skirts, the pattern of plaids,
The walnut frames of the mirrors
Amazed by Karenina's beauty,
And in the narrow hall the wallpaper
We feasted our eyes on in our childhood
By the yellow light of the kerosene lamp,
And the same plush on the armchairs . . .
      Everything out of order, rushed, somehow . . .
      Fathers and grandfathers incomprehensible.
      Lands mortgaged. And in Baden—roulette.

And a woman with translucent eyes
(Of such deep blue that to gaze into them
And not think of the sea was impossible),
With the rarest of names and white hands,
And a kindness that as an inheritance
I have from her, it seems—
Useless gift for my harsh life . . .

The country shivers, and the convict from Omsk
Understood everything and made the sign of the cross over it all.
Now he shuffles everything around

And, over this primordial chaos,
Like some kind of spirit, he rises. Midnight sounds.
His pen squeaks, and page after page
Stinks of Semyonov Square.

This is when we decided to be born,
And timing it perfectly
So as not to miss any of those pageants
Yet to come, we bid farewell to non-existence.

September 3, 1940
Leningrad
October 1943
Tashkent

SECOND

So here it is—that autumn landscape
Of which I've been so frightened all my life:
And the sky—like a flaming abyss
And the sounds of the city—heard as if
From another world, forever strange:
It's as if everything I've struggled with inside myself
All my life received its own life
And bodied forth in these
Blind walls, in this black garden . . .
And right now, over my shoulder,
My old house still spies on me

With its squinting, disapproving eye,
That omnipresent window.
Fifteen years—pretending to be
Fifteen granite centuries,
But I myself was like granite:
Now beg, suffer, summon
The queen of the sea. It doesn't matter. No need to . . .
But I should have convinced myself
That all this has happened many times,
And not to me alone—to others too,
And even worse. No, not worse—better.
And my voice—and this, really,
Was the most frightening—uttered from the darkness:
"Fifteen years ago, with what rejoicing
You greeted this day, you begged the heavens
And the choirs of stars and the choirs of oceans
To salute the glorious meeting
With the one you left today . . .

So this is your silver anniversary:
Summon the guests, stand in splendor, celebrate!"

March 1942, Tashkent

THIRD

Blessed is he who visits this world
At his appointed hour.—TYUTCHEV

N.A.O.

I, like a river,
Was rechanneled by this stern age.
They gave me a substitute life. It began to flow
In a different course, passing the other one,
And I do not recognize my banks.
Oh, how many spectacles I've missed,
And the curtain rose without me
And then fell. How many of my friends
I've never met once in my life,
And how many cities' skylines
Could have drawn tears from my eyes;
But I only know one city in the world
And I could find my way around it in my sleep.
And how many poems I didn't write,
And their mysterious chorus prowls around me,
And, perhaps, may yet somehow
Strangle me . . .
I am aware of beginnings and endings,
And life after the end, and something
That I don't have to remember just now.
And some other woman occupied
The special place reserved for me
And bears my legal name,

Leaving me the nickname, with which
I did, probably, everything that could be done.
I will not lie down, alas, in my own grave.
But sometimes the playful spring wind
Or the combination of words in some book,
Or somebody's smile suddenly drags
Me into that life that never took place.
In this year, such and such would have happened,
In that year—that: traveling, seeing, thinking
And remembering, and entering into a new love
As into a mirror, with dim awareness
Of betrayal and of the wrinkle
That wasn't there the day before.
. . . .
But had I observed from there
The life I am living today,
I would finally discover envy . . .

September 2, 1945
Leningrad

FOURTH

> *The last key—is the cold key of oblivion.*
> *It gives sweeter satisfaction than all the ardors*
> *of the heart.*—PUSHKIN

There are three ages to memories,
And the first—is like just yesterday.

The soul is under their blissful arch,
And the body basks in their blissful shade.
Laughter has not yet died, tears flow,
The ink blot on the desk has not faded—
And, like a seal on the heart, the kiss,
Unique, valedictory, unforgettable . . .
But this does not long endure . . .
Already there is no arch overhead, but somewhere
In a remote suburb, a solitary house,
Where it is cold in winter, hot in summer,
Where there are spiders, and dust on everything,
Where ardent letters are decomposing,
Portraits are stealthily changing.
People walk to this house as if to their grave,
And wash their hands with soap when they return,
And blink away a facile tear
From weary eyes—and breathe out heavy sighs . . .
But the clock ticks, one springtime is superseded
By another, the sky glows pink,
Names of cities change
And there are no remaining witnesses to the events,
And no one to weep with, no one to remember with.
And slowly the shades withdraw from us,
Shades we no longer call back,
Whose return would be too terrible for us.
And waking one morning we realize that we have forgotten
Even the path to that solitary house,
And, choking with anger and shame,
We run there, but (as it happens in dreams),

Everything has changed: the people, the objects, the walls,
And nobody knows us—we are strangers.
We don't find ourselves there . . . My God!
And then it is that bitterness wells up:
We realize that we couldn't have fit
That past into the boundaries of our life,
And that it is almost as foreign to us
As to our next-door neighbor,
That those who died we wouldn't recognize,
And those from whom God separated us
Got along perfectly well without us—and even
That everything turned out for the best . . .

February 5, 1945
Leningrad

FIFTH
ABOUT THE 1910'S

> *You—the conqueror of life,*
> *And I—your unfettered friend.*—N. GUMILYOV

And there was no rosy childhood . . .
Freckles and toy bears and curls,
And doting aunts and scary uncles, or even
Friends among the river pebbles.
I myself, from the very beginning,
Seemed to myself like someone's dream or delirium,

Or a reflection in someone else's mirror,
Without flesh, without meaning, without a name.
Already I knew the list of crimes
That I was destined to commit.
And so, wandering like a somnambulist,
I stepped into life and startled it:
It stretched before me like the meadow
Where once Proserpina strolled.
Before me, who was without family, unskilled,
Doors unexpectedly opened
And people streamed out and exclaimed:
"She came, she herself came!"
But I looked at them in astonishment
And I thought: "They must be mad!"
And the more they praised me,
The more people admired me,
The more frightful it was to live in the world,
And the more I yearned to awaken,
For I knew that I would pay dearly
In prison, in the grave, in the madhouse,
Wherever someone like me must awaken—
But the torture dragged on as good fortune.

July 4, 1955
Moscow

SIXTH

It was dreadful to live in that house,
And not the patriarchal glow of the hearth,
Not the cradle of my child,
Not the fact that we were both young
And full of ideas,
. . . . . and that good fortune
Didn't dare take a step from our door
For seven years,
Nothing diminished that feeling of fear.
And I learned to laugh at it,
And I left a drop of wine
And crumbs of bread for the one who every night
Scratched like a dog at the door
Or peered through the low-set window,
While we, keeping still, tried
Not to see what was happening behind the mirror,
Under whose heavy tread
The steps of the dark staircase groaned,
As if pleading dolefully for mercy,
And you said, smiling strangely:
"Who are *they* dragging down the stairs?"

Now that you're there, where everything is known—tell me:
What else lived in that house besides us?

1921
Tsarskoe Selo

SEVENTH

And I have been silent, silent for thirty years.
The silence of arctic ice
Stands through innumerable nights,
Closing in to snuff out my candle.
The dead are silent like this, but that's understandable
And not as horrible . . . .

My silence can be heard everywhere.
It fills the courtroom,
And it could have drowned out
The roar of rumor, and like a miracle
It puts its stamp on everything.
It is part of everything. O God!
Who could have thought up such a role for me?
Allow me for a moment, O Lord,
To begin to become a little bit like someone else.
. . . .
And could it be I haven't drunk hemlock?
So why didn't I die
As I should have—then and there?
. . . .
No, not to the one who is searching for these books,
Who stole them, who even bound them,
Who carries them around like secret chains,
Who memorized every syllable
. . . .
No, not to that one does my dream fly,
And not to that one will I give my blessing,

But only to the one who dared
To hoist my silence on a banner,
Who lived with it, and who believed in it,
Who took the measure of this pitch-dark, bottomless pit

. . . .

My silence is in music and in song
And in somebody's loathsome love,
In parting, in books . . .

        In what is least known
In the world . . . .

. . . .

I myself am sometimes afraid of it,
When with all its weight
It presses on me, breathing and drawing close:
There is no defense, or rather—there is nothing.
Who knows how it turned to stone.
You can imagine how it scorched my heart
And with what kind of fire. Whose concern is it?
Everyone feels so comfortable and accustomed to it.
All of you agree to share it,
Nevertheless it is always mine

. . . .

It is deforming my fate,
It almost devoured my soul,
But I will break it some day
To summon death to the whipping post.

1958–1964
Leningrad

RAFAEL ALBERTI
Translated from the Spanish by Mark Strand

Buster Keaton Looks in the Woods for His Love Who Is a Real Cow

1, 2, 3, 4,
My shoes don't fit in these four tracks.
If my shoes don't fit in these four tracks,
whose tracks are they?
A shark's?
A new-born elephant's? A duck's?
A flea's? A quail's?

(Yooo Hooo)

Georginaaaaaaaa!
Where are you?
I don't hear you, Georgina!
What will your father's mustache think of me?

(PaaaPaaaaa)

Georginaaaaaaaa!
Are you here or not?

Spruce, where is she?
Alder, where is she?
Pine, where is she?

Has Georgina come by here?

(Yooo Hooo, Yooo Hooo.)

She came by at one, munching grass.
Caw caw,
the crow was leading her on with some mignonette.
Wooo wooo,
the owl with a dead mouse.

Excuse me, gentlemen, but it makes me want to cry!
(Booo hooo, booo hooo.)

Georgina!
Now you are short only one horn
of acquiring a postman's cap and a doctorate
in the truly useful profession of cyclist.

(Cri, cri, cri, cri.)

Even the crickets pity me
and the tick shares my sorrow.
Pity him in the tuxedo who looks for you and cries for you
in one rainstorm after another,
the soft-hearted one, the one in the derby,
who worries about you among the trees.

Georginaaaaaaaaaaaaaaaaa!

(Mooooooooooooo.)

Are you a sweet child or a real cow?
My heart always told me that you were a real cow.

Your father, that you were a sweet child.
My heart, that you were a real cow.
A sweet child.
A real cow.
A child.
A cow.
A child or a cow?
Or a child and a cow?
I never found out.
                    Goodbye, Georgina.
                         (Bang!)

YEHUDA AMICHAI

Translated from the Hebrew by Benjamin and Barbara Harshav

We Have Done Our Duty

We did our duty.
We went out with our children
To gather mushrooms in the forest
Which we planted ourselves when we were children.

We learned the names of wildflowers
Whose aroma was
Like blood spilled in vain.
We laid a big love on small bodies,
We stood enlarged and shrunken in turn,
In the eyes of the holder of the binoculars,
Divine and mad.

And in the war of the sons of light and the sons of darkness
We loved the good and soothing darkness
And hated the painful light.
We did our duty,
We loved our children
More than our homeland,
We dug all the wells into the earth
And now we dig into the space of the skies,
Well after well, with no beginning, no end.

We did our duty,
The words *you shall remember* we changed to "we will forget"
As they change a bus schedule
When the direction of the route changes,
Or as they change the plaques

Of *Dew and Showers* and *He Who Brings Rain* in the synagogue
When the seasons change.

We did our duty,
We arranged our lives in flowerbeds and shadows
And straight paths, pleasant for walking,
Like the garden of a mental hospital.

Our despair is domesticated and gives us peace,
Only the hopes have remained,
Wild hopes, their screams
Shatter the night and rip up the day.

We did our duty.
We were like people entering a moviehouse,
Passing by those coming out, red-faced
Or pale, crying quietly or laughing aloud,
And they enter without a second glance, without
Turning back, into the light and the dark and the light.
We have done our duty.

A . R . A M M O N S

The City Limits

When you consider the radiance, that it does not withhold
itself but pours its abundance without selection into every
nook and cranny not overhung or hidden; when you consider

that birds' bones make no awful noise against the light but
lie low in the light as in a high testimony; when you consider
the radiance, that it will look into the guiltiest

swervings of the weaving heart and bear itself upon them,
not flinching into disguise or darkening; when you consider
the abundance of such resource as illuminates the glow-blue

bodies and gold-skeined wings of flies swarming the dumped
guts of a natural slaughter or the coil of shit and in no
way winces from its storms of generosity; when you consider

that air or vacuum, snow or shale, squid or wolf, rose or lichen,
each is accepted into as much light as it will take, then
the heart moves roomier, the man stands and looks about, the

leaf does not increase itself above the grass, and the dark
work of the deepest cells is of a tune with May bushes
and fear lit by the breadth of such calmly turns to praise.

CARLOS DRUMMOND DE ANDRADE

Translated from the Portuguese by Mark Strand

Residue

From everything a little remained.
From my fear. From your disgust.
From stifled cries. From the rose
a little remained.

A little remained of light
caught inside the hat.
In the eyes of the pimp
a little remained of tenderness,
very little.

A little remained of the dust
that covered your white shoes.
Of your clothes a little remained,
a few velvet rags, very
very few.

From everything a little remained.
From the bombed-out bridge,
from the two blades of grass,
from the empty pack
of cigarettes a little remained.

So from everything a little remains.
A little remains of your chin
in the chin of your daughter.

A little remained of your
blunt silence, a little
in the angry wall,
in the mute rising leaves.

A little remained from everything
in porcelain saucers,
in the broken dragon, in the white flowers,
in the creases of your brow,
in the portrait.

Since from everything a little remains,
why won't a little
of me remain? In the train
traveling north, in the ship,
in newspaper ads,
why not a little of me in London,
a little of me somewhere?
In a consonant?
In a well?
A little remains dangling
in the mouths of rivers,
just a little, and the fish
don't avoid it, which is very unusual.

From everything a little remains.
Not much: this absurd drop
dripping from the faucet,
half salt and half alcohol,

this frog leg jumping,
this watch crystal
broken into a thousand wishes,
this swan's neck,
this childhood secret . . .
From everything a little remained:
from me; from you; from Abelard.
Hair on my sleeve,
from everything a little remained;
wind in my ears,
burbing, rumbling
from an upset stomach,
and small artifacts:
bell jar, honeycomb, revolver
cartridge, aspirin tablet.

From everything a little remained.

And from everything a little remains.
Oh, open the bottles of lotion
and smother
the cruel, unbearable odor of memory.

Still, horribly, from everything a little remains,
under the rhythmic waves
under the clouds and the wind
under the bridges and under the tunnels
under the flames and under the sarcasm
under the phlegm and under the vomit

under the cry from the dungeon, the guy they forgot
under the spectacles and under the scarlet death
under the libraries, asylums, victorious churches
under yourself and under your feet already hard
under the ties of family, the ties of class,
from everything a little always remains.
Sometimes a button. Sometimes a rat.

MÁRIO DE ANDRADE
Translated from the Spanish by Jack E. Tomlins

Ode to the Bourgeois Gentleman

I insult the bourgeois! The money-grabbing bourgeois,
the bourgeois-bourgeois!
The well-made digestion of São Paulo!
The man-belly! The man-buttocks!
The man who being French, Brazilian, Italian,
is always a cautious little take-your-time!

I insult the cautious aristocracies!
The kerosene lamp barons! the count Johns! The jackass-braying
    dukes!
who live inside walls never scaled;
and lament the blood of a few puny pennies
to say that their lady's daughters speak French
and play the "Printemps" with their fingernails!

I insult the fatal-bourgeois!
The undigested beans and bacon, guardian of traditions!
Down with those who count out their tomorrows!
Behold the life of our Septembers!
Will the sun shine? Will it rain? Harlequinate!
But in the rain of the rose gardens
Ecstasy will always make the Sun shine!

Death to flabbiness!
Death to cerebral adiposities!
Death to the monthly-bourgeois!
to the movie-bourgeois! to the tillbury-bourgeois!
Swiss Bakery! Living death to the Café Adriano!
"Oh, sweetheart, what shall I give you for your birthday?"

"A necklace . . ." "Fifteen hundred bucks!!!
But we're starving to death!"

Eat! Oh, eat yourself up! stupefied gelatin!
Oh, moral mashed potatoes!
Oh, hairs in the nostrils! Oh, bald pates!
Hatred to regulated temperaments!
Hatred to muscular clocks! Death and infamy!
Hatred to calculation! Hatred to grocery stores!
Hatred to those without weakness or repentance,
ever and eternally the conventional samenesses!
Hands at their backs! I'll beat the rhythm! Hey!
Columns of two! First position! March!
All to the Main Jail of my inebriating rancor!

Hatred and execration! Hatred and rage! Hatred and more hatred!
Death to the bourgeois on his knees,
smelling of religion and not believing in God!
Scarlet hatred! Fecund hatred! Cyclical hatred!
Fundamental hatred, without pardon!

Down and away! Boo! Away with the good bourgeois gentleman! . . .

ALAN ANSEN

Fatness

1. How comely glisten the rounded cheeks and the swelling thighs! Blessed the sinews, auspicious the tissues that prosper to the benediction of amplitude.
2. Rejoice, ye beholders, in the nutritive steaks and comforting sauces, the delights of the palate and the strength-giving proteins.
3. The chiming bowels give thanks to their Maker and broadcast the incense of life lived well.
4. Bear witness, O body in bloom, to the goodness of the Lord and to the wealthiness with which He endowed thee.
5. The people dance in the streets, fulfilled with my fullness.
6. Just are the ways of God to men! A proof, let me communicate gladness.
7. In the day of my rising up, low I give thanks: Thou hast heaped up my treasure, Thou hast exalted my horn—to Thee be the glory.
8. Not for us alone, O Lord, not for us alone; but let Thy bounteousness extend to all: soften the hearts of the princes that they endue even the meanest, especially the meanest, with the fruits of benevolent earth.
9. I rest not from celebrating the goodness of the All-Highest: my heart never wearies in hymns of thanksgiving.
10. Grow to the height of blessing: there are giants on the face of the earth in these days.

BETH

11. Stately and calm, the mature body serene studies quietness.
12. The due and regular refection soothes the stomach with punctual beauty.
13. Punctual, too, the bowels' outpourings betoken the sanctity of the measured life.
14. Roseate repletion hallows my accomplished torso.
15. Solid in a world of solids, I exist a landmark to the more fluid.
16. Unshaken, I contemplate unmoved the variations of behavior.
17. My spirit, if it does not rejoice, it snoozes complacent.
18. Content you, turbulent minds, with the portion meted out to you: lest a worse thing befall.
19. Conform yourselves to the established rite: in a multitude of worships only the will is adored.
20. Peace! Peace! Let us imprecate peace on the living, the dead and the resting.

GIMEL

21. An inert mass groans to its Creator: can this dead fat live?
22. Shovel in the pork, the oils and the butters: so much the less for sneering starvelings.
23. Bowels, laboratories of decay, infect the unjudging air with the poison gases of your spiteful superfluity.
24. Sweaty flesh, gravid with itself, overlays my life.
25. Mine enemies hiss at me, a ridiculous monster, a laughable roadblock in the path of their impatience.

26. Their mockery I answer with my mightiest curse, my continued existence.
27. My vacuously frenzied spirit tears and rends in vain the meaty clogs of static adiposity.
28. Jacob, I lie immobilized in possession: why troublest thou thyself?
29. Beyond this bed and this trough is nothing: blind and deaf, I am conscious only of weight and pain.
30. Heaviness is all.

DALETH

31. Let us fly then, my corpulent soul, to the hot lands, the black lands, the simple and starved lands,
32. Where adoring the woolly-haired natives proclaim the steatopygous and the beautiful one.
33. Up! Up and away.

GUILLAUME APOLLINAIRE

Translated from the French by James Wright

The Pretty Redhead

I stand here in the sight of everyone a man full of sense
Knowing life and knowing of death what a living man can know
Having gone through the griefs and happinesses of love
Having known sometimes how to impose his ideas
Knowing several languages
Having travelled more than a little
Having seen war in the artillery and the infantry
Wounded in the head trepanned under chloroform
Having lost his best friends in the horror of battle

I know as much as one man alone can know
Of the ancient and the new
And without troubling myself about this war today
Between us and for us my friends
I judge this long quarrel between tradition and imagination
Between order and adventure

You whose mouth is made in the image of God's mouth
Mouth which is order itself
Judge kindly when you compare us
With those who were the very perfection of order
We who are seeking everywhere for adventure

We are not your enemies
Who want to give ourselves vast strange domains
Where mystery flowers into any hands that long for it
Where there are new fires colors never seen
A thousand fantasies difficult to make sense out of
They must be made real

All we want is to explore kindness the enormous country where
   everything is silent
And there is time which somebody can banish or welcome home
Pity for us who fight always on the frontiers
Of the illimitable and the future
Pity our mistakes pity our sins

Here summer is coming the violent season
And so my youth is as dead as spring
Oh Sun it is the time of reason grown passionate
And I am still waiting
To follow the forms she takes noble and gentle
So I may love her alone

She comes and draws me as a magnet draws filaments of iron
She has the lovely appearance
Of an adorable redhead
Her hair turns golden you would say
A beautiful lightning flash that goes on and on
Or the flames that spread out their feathers
In wilting tea roses

But laugh laugh at me
Men everywhere especially people from here
For there are so many things that I don't dare to tell you
So many things that you would not let me say
Have pity on me

Syringa

Orpheus liked the glad personal quality
Of the things beneath the sky. Of course, Eurydice was a part
Of this. Then one day, everything changed. He rends
Rocks into fissures with lament. Gullies, hummocks
Can't withstand it. The sky shudders from one horizon
To the other, almost ready to give up wholeness.
Then Apollo quietly told him: "Leave it all on earth.
Your lute, what point? Why pick at a dull pavan few care to
Follow, except a few birds of dusty feather,
Not vivid performances of the past." But why not?
All other things must change too.
The seasons are no longer what they once were,
But it is the nature of things to be seen only once,
As they happen along, bumping into other things, getting along
Somehow. That's where Orpheus made his mistake.
Of course Eurydice vanished into the shade;
She would have even if he hadn't turned around.
No use standing there like a gray stone toga as the whole wheel
Of recorded history flashes past, struck dumb, unable to utter an
    intelligent
Comment on the most thought-provoking element in its train.
Only love stays on the brain, and something these people,
These other ones, call life. Singing accurately
So that the notes mount straight up out of the well of
Dim noon and rival the tiny, sparkling yellow flowers
Growing around the brink of the quarry, encapsulizes
The different weights of the things.
                                        But it isn't enough

To just go on singing. Orpheus realized this
And didn't mind so much about his reward being in heaven
After the Bacchantes had torn him apart, driven
Half out of their minds by his music, what it was doing to them.
Some say it was for his treatment of Eurydice.
But probably the music had more to do with it, and
The way music passes, emblematic
Of life and how you cannot isolate a note of it
And say it is good or bad. You must
Wait till it's over. "The end crowns all,"
Meaning also that the "tableau"
Is wrong. For although memories, of a season, for example,
Melt into a single snapshot, one cannot guard, treasure
That stalled moment. It too is flowing, fleeting;
It is a picture of flowing, scenery, though living, mortal,
Over which an abstract action is laid out in blunt,
Harsh strokes. And to ask more than this
Is to become the tossing reeds of that slow,
Powerful stream, the trailing grasses
Playfully tugged at, but to participate in the action
No more than this. Then in the lowering gentian sky
Electric twitches are faintly apparent first, then burst forth
Into a shower of fixed, cream-colored flares. The horses
Have each seen a share of the truth, though each thinks,
"I'm a maverick. Nothing of this is happening to me,
Though I can understand the language of birds, and
The itinerary of the lights caught in the storm is fully apparent
    to me.

Their jousting ends in music much
As trees move more easily in the wind after a summer storm
And is happening in lacy shadows of shore-trees, now, day after
    day."

But how late to be regretting all this, even
Bearing in mind that regrets are always late, too late!
To which Orpheus, a bluish cloud with white contours,
Replies that these are of course not regrets at all,
Merely a careful, scholarly setting down of
Unquestioned facts, a record of pebbles along the way.
And no matter how all this disappeared,
Or got where it was going, it is no longer
Material for a poem. Its subject
Matters too much, and not enough, standing there helplessly
While the poem streaked by, its tail afire, a bad
Comet screaming hate and disaster, but so turned inward
That the meaning, good or other, can never
Become known. The singer thinks
Constructively, builds up his chant in progressive stages
Like a skyscraper, but at the last minute turns away.
The song is engulfed in an instant in blackness
Which must in turn flood the whole continent
With blackness, for it cannot see. The singer
Must then pass out of sight, not even relieved
Of the evil burthen of the words. Stellification
Is for the few, and comes about much later
When all record of these people and their lives
Has disappeared into libraries, onto microfilm.

A few are still interested in them. "But what about
So-and-so?" is still asked on occasion. But they lie
Frozen and out of touch until an arbitrary chorus
Speaks of a totally different incident with a similar name
In whose tale are hidden syllables
Of what happened so long before that
In some small town, one indifferent summer.

W. H. AUDEN

In Memory of W. B. Yeats

(d. Jan. 1939)

I

He disappeared in the dead of winter:
The brooks were frozen, the airports almost deserted,
And snow disfigured the public statues;
The mercury sank in the mouth of the dying day.
O all the instruments agree
The day of his death was a dark cold day.

Far from his illness
The wolves ran on through the evergreen forests,
The peasant river was untempted by the fashionable quays;
By mourning tongues
The death of the poet was kept from his poems.

But for him it was his last afternoon as himself,
An afternoon of nurses and rumours;
The provinces of his body revolted,
The squares of his mind were empty,
Silence invaded the suburbs,
The current of his feeling failed: he became his admirers.

Now he is scattered among a hundred cities
And wholly given over to unfamiliar affections;
To find his happiness in another kind of wood
And be punished under a foreign code of conscience.
The words of a dead man
Are modified in the guts of the living.

But in the importance and noise of tomorrow
When the brokers are roaring like beasts on the floor of the Bourse,
And the poor have the sufferings to which they are fairly accustomed,
And each in the cell of himself is almost convinced of his freedom;
A few thousand will think of this day
As one thinks of a day when one did something slightly unusual.

O all the instruments agree
The day of his death was a dark cold day.

2

You were silly like us: your gift survived it all;
The parish of rich women, physical decay,
Yourself; mad Ireland hurt you into poetry.
Now Ireland has her madness and her weather still,
For poetry makes nothing happen: it survives
In the valley of its saying where executives
Would never want to tamper; it flows south
From ranches of isolation and the busy griefs,
Raw towns that we believe and die in; it survives,
A way of happening, a mouth.

3

Earth, receive an honoured guest:
William Yeats is laid to rest.
Let the Irish vessel lie
Emptied of its poetry.

In the nightmare of the dark
All the dogs of Europe bark,
And the living nations wait,
Each sequestered in its hate;

Intellectual disgrace
Stares from every human face,
And the seas of pity lie
Locked and frozen in each eye.

Follow, poet, follow right
To the bottom of the night,
With your unconstraining voice
Still persuade us to rejoice;

With the farming of a verse
Make a vineyard of the curse,
Sing of human unsuccess
In a rapture of distress;

In the deserts of the heart
Let the healing fountain start,
In the prison of his days
Teach the free man how to praise.

INGEBORG BACHMANN

Translated from the German by Peter Filkins

To the Sun

More beautiful than the remarkable moon and its noble light,
More beautiful than the stars, the celebrated orders of night,
Much more beautiful than the fiery display of a comet,
And so much more beautiful than any planet,
Because your life and my life depend on it daily, is the sun.

Beautiful sun, which rises, remembering its tasks
And completing them, most beautiful in summer, when a day
Shimmers on the coast and the calm mirror of sails
Passes before your eye, until you tire and eventually doze.

Without the sun, even art puts on a veil again.
You cease to appear to me, and the sea and the sand,
Lashed by shadows, hide beneath my lids.

Beautiful light, which keeps us warm, sustains and marvelously
    ensures
That I see again, and that I see you again!

Nothing more beautiful under the sun than to be under the sun . . .

Nothing more beautiful than to see the reed in the water and the
    bird above
Pondering its flight and, below, the fish in their school,
Colorful, shapely, come into the world on a beam of light,
And to see the circumference, the square of a field, the thousand
    corners of my land,
And the dress you have put on. Your dress, bell-shaped and blue!

A beautiful blue in which peacocks strut and bow,
The blue of distances, zones of joy with climates for my every
   mood.
The horizon's blue chance! And my enchanted eyes
Widen again and blink and burn themselves sore.

Beautiful sun, which even from dust deserves the highest praise,
Causing me to raise a cry, not to the moon,
The stars, the night's garish comets that name me a fool,
But rather to you, and ultimately to you alone,
As I lament the inevitable loss of my sight.

JOHN BERRYMAN

The Moon and the Night and the Men

On the night of the Belgian surrender the moon rose
Late, a delayed moon, and a violent moon
For the English or the American beholder;
The French beholder. It was a cold night,
People put on their wraps, the troops were cold
No doubt, despite the calendar, no doubt
Numbers of refugees coughed, and the sight
Or sound of some killed others. A cold night.

On Outer Drive there was an accident:
A stupid well-intentioned man turned sharp
Right and abruptly he became an angel
Fingering an unfamiliar harp,
Or screamed in hell, or was nothing at all.
Do not imagine this is unimportant.
He was a part of the night, part of the land,
Part of the bitter and exhausted ground
Out of which memory grows.

                        Michael and I
Stared at each other over chess, and spoke
As little as possible, and drank and played.
The chessmen caught in the European eye,
Neither of us I think had a free look
Although the game was fair. The move one made
It was difficult at last to keep one's mind on.
"Hurt and unhappy" said the man in London.
We said to each other, The time is coming near
When none shall have books or music, none his dear,

And only a fool will speak aloud his mind.
History is approaching a speechless end,
As Henry Adams said. Adams was right.

All this occurred on the night when Leopold
Fulfilled the treachery four years before
Begun—or was he well-intentioned, more
Roadmaker to hell than king? At any rate,
The moon came up late and the night was cold,
Many men died—although we know the fate
Of none, nor of anyone, and the war
Goes on, and the moon in the breast of man is cold.

ELIZABETH BISHOP

In the Waiting Room

In Worcester, Massachusetts,
I went with Aunt Consuelo
to keep her dentist's appointment
and sat and waited for her
in the dentist's waiting room.
It was winter. It got dark
early. The waiting room
was full of grown-up people,
arctics and overcoats,
lamps and magazines.
My aunt was inside
what seemed like a long time
and while I waited I read
the *National Geographic*
(I could read) and carefully
studied the photographs:
the inside of a volcano,
black, and full of ashes;
then it was spilling over
in rivulets of fire.
Osa and Martin Johnson
Dressed in riding breeches,
laced boots, and pith helmets.
A dead man slung on a pole
—"Long Pig," the caption said.
Babies with pointed heads
wound round and round with string;
black, naked women with necks
wound round and round with wire

like the necks of light bulbs.
Their breasts were horrifying.
I read it right straight through.
I was too shy to stop.
And then I looked at the cover:
the yellow margins, the date.

Suddenly, from inside,
came an *oh!* of pain
—Aunt Consuelo's voice—
not very loud or long.
I wasn't at all surprised;
even then I knew she was
a foolish, timid woman.
I might have been embarrassed,
but wasn't. What took me
completely by surprise
was that it was *me:*
my voice, in my mouth.
Without thinking at all
I was my foolish aunt,
I—we—were falling, falling,
our eyes glued to the cover
of the *National Geographic*,
February, 1918.

I said to myself: three days
and you'll be seven years old.
I was saying it to stop

the sensation of falling off
the round, turning world
into cold, blue-black space.
But I felt: you are an *I*,
you are an *Elizabeth*,
you are one of *them*.
Why should you be one, too?
I scarcely dared to look
to see what it was I was.
I gave a sidelong glance
—I couldn't look any higher—
at shadowy gray knees,
trousers and skirts and boots
and different pairs of hands
lying under the lamps.
I knew that nothing stranger
had ever happened, that nothing
stranger could ever happen.

Why should I be my aunt,
or me, or anyone?
What similarities—
boots, hands, the family voice
I felt in my throat, or even
the *National Geographic*
and those awful hanging breasts—
held us all together
or made us all just one?
How—I didn't know any

word for it—how "unlikely" . . .
How had I come to be here,
like them, and overhear
a cry of pain that could have
got loud and worse but hadn't?

The waiting room was bright
and too hot. It was sliding
beneath a big black wave,
another, and another.

Then I was back in it.
The War was on. Outside,
in Worcester, Massachusetts,
were night and slush and cold,
and it was still the fifth
of February, 1918.

Evening in the Sanitarium*

The free evening fades, outside the windows fastened with decora-
tive iron grilles.
The lamps are lighted; the shades drawn; the nurses are watching
a little.
It is the hour of the complicated knitting on the safe bone needles;
of the games of anagrams and bridge;
The deadly game of chess; the book held up like a mask.

The period of the wildest weeping, the fiercest delusion, is over.
The women rest their tired half-healed hearts; they are almost well.
Some of them will stay almost well always: the blunt-faced woman
whose thinking dissolved
Under academic discipline; the manic-depressive girl
Now leveling off; one paranoiac afflicted with jealousy.
Another with persecution. Some alleviation has been possible.

O fortunate bride, who never again will become elated after child-
birth!
O lucky older wife, who has been cured of feeling unwanted!
To the suburban railway station you will return, return,
To meet forever Jim home on the 5:35.
You will be again as normal and selfish and heartless as anybody else.

There is life left: the piano says it with its octave smile.
The soft carpets pad the thump and splinter of the suicide to be.
Everything will be splendid: the grandmother will not drink
habitually.

*This poem was originally published with the subtitle "Imitated from Auden."

The fruit salad will bloom on the plate like a bouquet
And the garden produce the blue-ribbon aquilegia.

The cats will be glad; the fathers feel justified; the mothers
    relieved.
The sons and husbands will no longer need to pay the bills.
Childhoods will be put away, the obscene nightmare abated.

At the ends of the corridors the baths are running.
Mrs. C. again feels the shadow of the obsessive idea.
Miss R. looks at the mantel-piece, which must mean something.

JORGE LUIS BORGES

Translated from the Spanish by Hoyt Rogers

In Praise of Darkness

Old age (the name that others give it)
can be the time of our greatest bliss.
The animal has died or almost died.
The man and his spirit remain.
I live among vague, luminous shapes
that are not darkness yet.
Buenos Aires,
whose edges disintegrated
into the endless plain,
has gone back to being the Recoleta, the Retiro,
the nondescript streets of the Once,
and the rickety old houses
we still call the South.
In my life there were always too many things.
Democritus of Abdera plucked out his eyes in order to think:
Time has been my Democritus.
This penumbra is slow and does not pain me;
it flows down a gentle slope,
resembling eternity.
My friends have no faces,
women are what they were so many years ago,
these corners could be other corners,
there are no letters on the pages of books.
All this should frighten me,
but it is a sweetness, a return.
Of the generations of texts on earth
I will have read only a few—
the ones that I keep reading in my memory,
reading and transforming.

From South, East, West, and North
the paths converge that have led me
to my secret center.
Those paths were echoes and footsteps,
women, men, death-throes, resurrections,
days and nights,
dreams and half-wakeful dreams,
every inmost moment of yesterday
and all the yesterdays of the world,
the Dane's staunch sword and the Persian's moon,
the acts of the dead,
shared love, and words,
Emerson and snow, so many things.
Now I can forget them. I reach my center,
my algebra and my key,
my mirror.
Soon I will know who I am.

C . P . C A V A F Y
Translated from the Greek by Edmund Keeley and Philip Sherrard

Waiting for the Barbarians

What are we waiting for, packed in the forum?

    The barbarians are due here today.

Why isn't anything going on in the senate?
Why have the senators given up legislating?

    Because the barbarians are coming today.
    What's the point of senators and their laws now?
    When the barbarians get here, they'll do the legislating.

Why did our emperor set out so early
to sit on his throne at the city's main gate,
in state, wearing the crown?

    Because the barbarians are coming today
    and the emperor's waiting to receive their leader.
    He's even got a citation to give him,
    loaded with titles and imposing names.

Why have our two consuls and praetors shown up today
wearing their embroidered, their scarlet togas?
Why have they put on bracelets with so many amethysts,
rings sparkling with all those emeralds?
Why are they carrying elegant canes
so beautifully worked in silver and gold?

    Because the barbarians are coming today
    and things like that dazzle barbarians.

And why don't our distinguished orators push forward as usual
to make their speeches, say what they have to say?

    Because the barbarians are coming today
    and they're bored by rhetoric and public speaking.

Why this sudden bewilderment, this confusion?
(How serious everyone looks.)
Why are the streets and squares rapidly emptying,
everyone going home so lost in thought?

    Because it's night and the barbarians haven't come.
    And some people just in from the border say
    there are no barbarians any longer.

Now what's going to happen to us without them?
The barbarians were a kind of solution.

PAUL CELAN

Translated from the German by Michael Hamburger

Death Fugue

Black milk of daybreak we drink it at sundown
we drink it at noon in the morning we drink it at night
we drink and we drink it
we dig a grave in the breezes there one lies unconfined
A man lives in the house he plays with the serpents he writes
he writes when dusk falls to Germany your golden hair Margarete
he writes it and steps out of doors and the stars are flashing he
    whistles his pack out
he whistles his Jews out in earth has them dig for a grave
he commands us strike up for the dance

Black milk of daybreak we drink you at night
we drink in the morning at noon we drink you at sundown
we drink and we drink you
A man lives in the house he plays with the serpents he writes
he writes when dusk falls to Germany your golden hair Margarete
your ashen hair Shulamith we dig a grave in the breezes there one
    lies unconfined

He calls out jab deeper into the earth you lot you others sing now
    and play
he grabs at the iron in his belt he waves it his eyes are blue
jab deeper you lot with your spades you others play on for the
    dance

Black milk of daybreak we drink you at night
we drink you at noon in the morning we drink you at sundown
we drink and we drink you
a man lives in the house your golden hair Margarete

your ashen hair Shulamith he plays with the serpents
He calls out more sweetly play death death is a master from
    Germany
he calls out more darkly now stroke your strings then as smoke you
    will rise into air
then a grave you will have in the clouds there one lies unconfined

Black milk of daybreak we drink you at night
we drink you at noon death is a master from Germany
we drink you at sundown and in the morning we drink and we
    drink you
death is a master from Germany his eyes are blue
he strikes you with leaden bullets his aim is true
a man lives in the house your golden hair Margarete
he sets his pack on to us he grants us a grave in the air
he plays with the serpents and daydreams death is a master from
    Germany

your golden hair Margarete
your ashen hair Shulamith

MENUS

I.

Truffled green turtle liver
Lobster Mexican
Florida pheasant
Iguana with Caribbean sauce
Gumbo and palmetto

II.

Red River salmon
Canadian bear ham
Roast beef from the meadows of Minnesota
Smoked eel
San Francisco tomatoes
Pale ale and California wine

III.

Winnipeg salmon
Scottish leg of lamb
Royal Canadian apples
Old French wines

IV.

Kankal oysters
Lobster salad celery hearts
French snails vanillaed in sugar
Kentucky fried chicken
Desserts coffee Canadian Club whiskey

V.

Pickled shark fins
Stillborn dog in honey
Rice wine with violets
Cream of silkworm cocoon
Salted earthworms and Kava liqueur
Seaweed jam

VI.

Canned beef from Chicago and German delicatessen
Crayfish
Pineapples guavas loquats coconuts mangoes custard apple
Baked breadfruit

VII.

Turtle soup
Fried oysters
Truffled bear paws
Lobster Javanese

VIII.

River crab and pimento stew
Suckling pig ringed with fried bananas
Hedgehog ravensara
Fruit

Traveling 1887–1923

A I M É C É S A I R E

Translated from the French by Clayton Eshleman and Annette Smith

Batouque*

The rice fields of cigarette butts of spit on the strange summons
of my simplicity are tattooing themselves with sharp peaks.
Floodgate open, the words perforated in my saliva
paler above the cities, resurface as cities
O transparent cities mounted on yaks
slow blood pissing the last memory into filigreed leaves
the boulevard bruised comet brusque crossed bird
strikes itself right in the sky
drowned in arrows
It's my kind of night most hollow and most null
a fan of compass fingers collapsed into the white laughter of
      slumbers.

batouque
once the world is naked and russet
like a womb burned to a cinder by the great suns of love
batouque
once the world is without inquest
a wondrous heart where the scenery of glances
splintered to bits is embossed
for the first time

once the attractions entrap the stars
once love and death are
a single coral snake resoldered around a gemless arm
without soot
without defense

*Batouque: Brazilian tom-tom rhythm

batouque of the river swollen with crocodile tears and drifting
    whips
batouque of the serpent tree of the dancers of the prairie
Pennsylvania roses peep at the eyes at the nose at the ears
at the windows of the tortured man's
sawed head
batouque of the woman with arms made of sea her hair an under-
    water source
rigor mortis turns bodies
into tears of steel
all the leafy phasmas make a sea of blue yuccas and rafts
all the neurotic phantasms have taken the bit between their teeth

batouque
once the world is turned into seduced abstraction
into shoots of rock salt
into the gardens of the sea
for the first and the last time
the mast of a forgotten caravel blazes an almond tree in the
    wreckage
a coco-palm a baobab a sheet of paper
the dismissal of an appeal
batouque
once the world is a strip mine
once the world from the height of the upper bridge is
my desire
your desire
conjugated in a leap into the inhaled void
under the awning of our eyes unfurls

all the sundust thronged with parachutes
with deliberate fires with oriflammes of red wheat
batouque of rotted eyes
batouque of molasses eyes
batouque of a doleful sea encrusted with islands
the Congo is a leap of sun raising at the end of a thread
a pail of bloody cities
a tuft of citronella in the wrenched open night
batouque
once the world is a tower of silence
when we are prey and vulture
all the rains of parrots
all the resignations of chinchillas
batouque of broken trumpets of an oily eyelid of virulent plovers
batouque of the rain killed split finely by reddened ears
purulence and vigilance

having raped to the point of transparency the narrow sex of the
    dusk
the tall Negro of the morning
to the depths of the cracked stone sea
takes on the hunger fruit of knotted cities
batouque
Oh! over the intimate void
—spurted spurting—
to the very rage of the site
the injunctions of a severe blood!
and the ship flew over the crater at the very threshold of the eagle
    plowed hour

the ship walked in calm boots of shooting stars
in wild boots of chopped off wharves and dress armor
and the ship let fly a volley of mice
of telegrams of cowries of houris
a Wolof dancer was dancing on points and signaling
from the point of the highest mast
all night long he was seen dancing laden with amulets and alcohol
bounding to the level of the fattened stars
an army of ravens
an army of knives
an army of parabolas
and the arched ship let fly an army of horses
At midnight the earth entered the channel of the crater
and the diamond wind hung with red cassocks
out of oblivion
blew the hooves of horses singing the adventure of milky voiced
    death
over the gardens of the carob planted rainbow

batouque
once the world is a breeding pond where I angle for my eyes on the
    line of your eyes
batouque
once the world is the far-sailing latex drunk from the flesh of sleep
batouque
batouque of swells and hiccups
batouque of sneered sobs
batouque of startled buffaloes
batouque of defiances of carmined wasp nests

in the pilfering of the fire and the smoking sky
batouque of hands
batouque of breasts
batouque of the seven beheadly sins
batouque of the sex with a bird-like peck a fish-like flight
batouque of a black princess in a diadem of melting sun
batouque of the princess stoking up a thousand unknown
    guardians
a thousand gardens forgotten under the sand and the rainbow
batouque of the princess with thighs like the Congo
like Borneo
like Casamance

batouque of night without a seed pit
of night without lips
cravatted by the jetsam of my nameless slave galley
by my boomerang bird
I threw my eye into the rolling into the guinea of despair and death
all strangeness solidifies Easter Island Easter Island
all strangeness cut off from the cavalries of darkness
a fresh brook flows in my hand a sargasso of melted screams

And the stripped-down ship dug my thirst-for-branches-minaret-
    exile
out of the brain of stubborn nights
batouque
the currents churned wisps of silver sabers
and nausea spoons
and the wind pierced by SOLAR fingers
sheared with fire the armpits of foam haired islands

batouque of pregnant lands
batouque of enwalled sea
batouque of humped hamlets of rotten feet of deaths spelled out in
    the priceless despair of memory
Basse-Pointe Diamant Tartant and Caravelle
gold shekels flotation planes assailed by sheaves and earcockles
sad brains crawled by orgasms
smoky armadillos
O the krumen teasers of my surf!
the sun has leapt from the great marsupial pouches of the dormer-
    less sea
into the full algebra of false hair and tramwayless rails
batouque the rivers fissure in the unlaced helmet of ravines
the sugar cane capsizes in the rolling of the earth swollen with
    she-camel humps
the coves smash at the ebbless bladders of stone with irresponsible
    lights

sun, go for their throats!
black howler black butcher black corsair batouque bedecked with
    spices and flies
Sleepy herd of mares under the bamboo thicket
bleed bleed herd of carambas

Assassin I acquit you in the name of rape.
I acquit you in the name of the Holy Ghost
I acquit you with my salamander hands
the day will pass like a wave with its bandoleer of cities
in its beggar's sack of powder-swollen shells

Sun sun russet serpent-eater leaning on my trances of a swamp in
    labor
the river of grass snakes that I call my veins
the river of battlements that I call my blood
the river of assagais that men call my face
the river of walking around the world
shall strike the Artesian rock with a hundred monsoon stars

Liberty my only pirate water of the New Year my only thirst
love my only sampan
we shall slip our calabash fingers of laughter
between the icy teeth of the Sleeping Beauty.

INGER CHRISTENSEN
Translated from the Danish by Susanna Nied

Poem on Death

nothing has happened
    for days I sit
        before the sheet of paper but
            nothing happens

*

I am like a child fed
    on sorrow
        I lift my arm
            but can write nothing

I am like a bird that
    has forgotten its kind
        I open my beak
            but can sing nothing

*

it feels so odd
    immodest to think
        about death when no one
            you know has died

it means that each time
    you look at yourself in the mirror
        you look death in the eye
            without crying

like a clear and fully
        comprehensible answer
                but to questions
                        you dare not ask

*

I can write nothing
        the sheet of paper empty as yesterday
                it seems so introverted
                        whitish and still

the same whitish color
        as snow grown old
                when the crust cracks
                        but nothing trickles out

nothing no tear
        no snowdrop nothing
                what if we did not
                        have to die

what if we always
        could be here on the earth
                which earthly condition
                        would we call death then

and which death call life
      when the blind person's soul
            has turned out the whites
                of its eyes and sees

*

last night I dreamed
      that I died and came running
            with my dog
                into the kingdom of death

there was no one to be seen
      just stones a few bushes
            a landscape that travelers
                have often told of

as I said, I was dead
      but so tired that I soon
            fell asleep on a boulder
                and dreamed I died again

I preferred not to die
      here in death's darkness
            but in my own home
                where I had not died

so on the way back
      I stopped at the boulder
            for days I sat and
                  wrote like this

all the death
      that an ordinary person
            must go through
                  in the course of life

when I awoke I saw
      that nothing had happened
            the sheet of paper empty
                  but I breathed easily

*

it is lonely to think
      of death I December
            with the clouds shrouding
                  your house

in the park the threatening
      light beneath the trees
            all kinds of dead people
                  wandering the town

one with a fish
    that he sorrows over
        like a helpless thing
            with tears of fishermen

one with the suffering
    bird that he carries
        over his heart
            his deceased heart

one with a word
    that has lost its object
        the surviving words
            that the body shakes off

the body whose blood
    runs away from its brain
        the body whose heart
            is cold as a knife

trapped
    between the stars
        we cry out
            from the coffin

words die
    on our lips
        the body is an animal
            that must die

in wild sorrow
        I suddenly remember
                the garden of Eden
                        the open wounds of graves

the zinc-plated watering can
        the metal vase the rake behind the stone
                and the autumn sigh of starlings
                        in gusts through the air

the sigh in which the worlds
        of the dead and not-dead
                meet in the comfort
                        of the great desolation

*

write of death
        describe in poem
                what you feel
                        about death

in the face of death
        I am like an animal
                and the animal can die
                        but can write nothing

try to write
    a poem about death
        has death a meaning
           what

now that apples
    fall so far
        from the tree of knowledge
          that they are not

eaten for pleasure
    nor from hunger
        but from weary greed
          death is alone

now that apples look like
    models of apples
        ideal-apples
          spotless

now that worms must gnaw
    at the breast of something
        other than children of man
          death is edged out

take death by the hand
    give it an apple
        walk up to its grave
          bite the apple first yourself

dance on its grave
      let wisdom rule
            devour layers of darkness
                  followed by sunlight

words do die like flies
      their bodies everywhere swept
            from the white sheet of paper
                  give dirt a little room

the newborn is like
      an ethereal creature
            not until stricken
                  with illness does it seem

a human child
      give us room to love
            a mortal form
                of immortality

as depth lifts water
      up to a spring
            death lifts the living
                up to drink

Marine Surface, Low Overcast

Out of churned aureoles
this buttermilk, this
herringbone of albatross,
floss of mercury,
déshabille of spun
aluminum, furred with a velouté
of looking-glass,

a stuff so single
it might almost be lifted,
folded over, crawled underneath
or slid between, as nakedness-
caressing sheets, or donned
and worn, the train-borne
trapping of an unrepeatable
occasion,

this wind-silver
rumpling as of oatfields,
a suede of meadow,
a nub, a nap, a mane of lustre
lithe as the slide
of muscle in its
sheath of skin,

laminae of living tissue,
mysteries of flex,
affinities of texture,
subtleties of touch, of pressure

and release, the suppleness
of long and intimate
association,

new synchronies of fingertip,
of breath, of sequence,
entities that still can rouse,
can stir or solder,
whip to a froth, or force
to march in strictly
hierarchical formation

down galleries of sheen, of flux,
cathedral domes that seem to hover
overturned and shaken like a basin
to the noise of voices,
from a rustle to the jostle
of such rush-hour
conglomerations

no loom, no spinneret, no forge, no factor,
no process whatsoever, patent
applied or not applied for,
no five-year formula, no fabric
for which pure imagining,
except thus prompted,
can invent the equal.

My Grandmother's Love Letters

There are no stars tonight
But those of memory.
Yet how much room for memory there is
In the loose girdle of soft rain.

There is even room enough
For the letters of my mother's mother,
Elizabeth,
That have been pressed so long
Into a corner of the roof
That they are brown and soft,
And liable to melt as snow.

Over the greatness of such space
Steps must be gentle.
It is all hung by an invisible white hair.
It trembles as birch limbs webbing the air.

And I ask myself:

"Are your fingers long enough to play
Old keys that are but echoes:
Is the silence strong enough
To carry back the music to its source
And back to you again
As though to her?"

Yet I would lead my grandmother by the hand
Through much of what she would not understand;
And so I stumble. And the rain continues on the roof
With such a sound of gently pitying laughter.

ROBERT DESNOS

Translated from the French by William Kulik with Carole Frankel

Mid-way

There's a precise moment in time
When a man reaches the exact middle of his life.
A fraction of a second
A fleeting bit of time, quicker than a glance
Quicker than a fit of passion,
Quicker than light.
And a man is aware of this moment.

Long avenues with overhanging trees stretch out
Towards a tower where a lady sleeps
Whose beauty resists kisses, the seasons,
Like a star the wind, like a rock the waves.

A quivering boat sinks bawling.
A flag blows at the top of a tree.
A well-dressed woman with stockings fallen to her ankles
Appears on a street corner
Flushed, trembling,
Protecting with her hand an old-fashioned lamp which is smoking.

And in addition a drunken stevedore sings in the corner of a bridge
And in addition a mistress bites the lips of her lover
And in addition a rose petal falls on an empty bed
And in addition three clocks toll the same hour
At several minute intervals
And in addition a man passing in the street comes back
Because someone has called his name
But it is not he this woman is calling.
And in addition a public official in full dress

Cramped by his shirttail wedged
   between his pants and his underwear
Dedicates an orphanage
And in addition a wonderful tomato falls from a truck speeding
Through the empty streets and rolls into the gutter
To be swept away later
And in addition a fire breaks out on the seventh floor of a building
And burns in the heart of the silent and indifferent city
And in addition a man hears a long forgotten song
which he will forget again
And in addition many other things
Many other things a man sees at the precise moment of the middle
   of his life
Many other things happen for a long time
   in the briefest of brief instants on earth.
He ponders the mystery of that second, that fraction of a second,

But he says, "Let's get rid of dark thoughts"
And he gets rid of them.
And what could he say?
And what better could he do?

Les Sans Cou

H . D .

The Helmsman

O be swift—
we have always known you wanted us.

We fled inland with our flocks.
we pastured them in hollows,
cut off from the wind
and the salt track of the marsh.
We worshipped inland—
we stepped past wood-flowers,
we forgot your tang,
we brushed wood-grass.

We wandered from pine-hills
through oak and scrub-oak tangles,
we broke hyssop and bramble,
we caught flower and new bramble-fruit
in our hair: we laughed
as each branch whipped back,
we tore our feet in half buried rocks
and knotted roots and acorn-cups.

We forgot—we worshipped.
We parted green from green,
we sought further thickets.
we dipped our ankles
through leaf-mould and earth,
and wood and wood-bank enchanted us—
and the feel of the clefts in the bark.
and the slope between tree and tree—

and a slender path strung field to field
and wood to wood
and hill to hill
and the forest after it.

We forgot—for a moment
tree-resin, tree-bark,
sweat of a torn branch
were sweet to the taste.

We were enchanted with the fields.
the tufts of coarse grass
in the shorter grass—
we loved all this.

But now, our boat climbs—hesitates—drops—
climbs—hesitates—crawls back—
climbs—hesitates—
O be swift—
we have always known you wanted us.

ALAN DUGAN

On an East Wind from the Wars

The wind came in for several thousand miles all night
and changed the close lie of your hair this morning. It
has brought well-travelled sea-birds who forget
their passage, singing. Old songs from the old
battle- and burial-grounds seem new in new lands.
They have to do with spring as new in seeming as
the old air idling in your hair in fact. So new,
so ignorant of any weather not your own,
you like it, breathing in a wind that swept
the battlefields of their worst smells, and took the dead
unburied to the potter's field of air. For miles
they sweetened on the sea-spray, the foul washed off,
and what is left is spring to you, love, sweet,
the salt blown past your shoulder luckily. No
wonder your laugh rings like a chisel as it cuts
your children's new names in the tombstone of thin air.

ROBERT DUNCAN

This Place Rumored to Have Been Sodom

might have been.
Certainly these ashes might have been pleasures.
Pilgrims on their way to the Holy Places remark
this place. Isn't it plain to all
that these mounds were palaces? This was once
a city among men, a gathering together of spirit.
It was measured by the Lord and found wanting.

It was measured by the Lord and found wanting,
destroyd by the angels that inhabit longing.
Surely this is Great Sodom where such cries
as if men were birds flying up from the swamp
ring in our ears, where such fears that were once
desires walk, almost spectacular,
stalking the desolate circles, red eyed.

This place rumord to have been a City surely was,
separated from us by the hand of the Lord.
The devout have laid out gardens in the desert,
drawn water from springs where the light was blighted.
How tenderly they must attend these friendships
or all is lost. All *is* lost.
Only the faithful hold this place green.

Only the faithful hold this place green
where the crown of fiery thorns descends.
Men that once lusted grow listless. A spirit
wrappd in a cloud, ashes more than ashes,
fire more than fire, ascends.

Only these new friends gather joyous here,
where the world like Great Sodom lies under fear.

The world like Great Sodom lies under Love
and knows not the hand of the Lord that moves.
This the friends teach where such cries
as if men were birds fly up from the crowds
gatherd and howling in the heat of the sun.
In the Lord Whom the friends have named at last Love
the images and loves of the friends never die.
This place rumord to have been Sodom is blessd
in the Lord's eyes.

The Love Song of J. Alfred Prufrock

S'io credessi che mia risposta fosse
a persona che mai tornasse al mondo,
questa fiamma staria senza più scosse.
Ma per ciò che giammai di questo fondo
non tornò vivo alcun, s'i'odo il vero,
senza tema d'infamia ti rispondo.

Let us go then, you and I,
When the evening is spread out against the sky
Like a patient etherised upon a table;
Let us go, through certain half-deserted streets,
The muttering retreats
Of restless nights in one-night cheap hotels
And sawdust restaurants with oyster-shells:
Streets that follow like a tedious argument
Of insidious intent
To lead you to an overwhelming question . . .
Oh, do not ask, "What is it?"
Let us go and make our visit.

    In the room the women come and go
Talking of Michelangelo.

    The yellow fog that rubs its back upon the window-panes,
The yellow smoke that rubs its muzzle on the window-panes,
Licked its tongue into the corners of the evening,
Lingered upon the pools that stand in drains,
Let fall upon its back the soot that falls from chimneys,
Slipped by the terrace, made a sudden leap,
And seeing that it was a soft October night,
Curled once about the house, and fell asleep.

And indeed there will be time
For the yellow smoke that slides along the street
Rubbing its back upon the window-panes;
There will be time, there will be time
To prepare a face to meet the faces that you meet;
There will be time to murder and create,
And time for all the works and days of hands
That lift and drop a question on your plate;
Time for you and time for me,
And time yet for a hundred indecisions,
And for a hundred visions and revisions,
Before the taking of a toast and tea.

In the room the women come and go
Talking of Michelangelo.

And indeed there will be time
To wonder, 'Do I dare?' and, 'Do I dare?'
Time to turn back and descend the stair,
With a bald spot in the middle of my hair—
(They will say: "How his hair is growing thin!")
My morning coat, my collar mounting firmly to the chin,
My necktie rich and modest, but asserted by a simple pin—
(They will say: "But how his arms and legs are thin!")
Do I dare
Disturb the universe?
In a minute there is time
For decisions and revisions which a minute will reverse.

For I have known them all already, known them all—
Have known the evenings, mornings, afternoons,
I have measured out my life with coffee spoons;
I know the voices dying with a dying fall
Beneath the music from a farther room.
    So how should I presume?

    And I have known the eyes already, known them all—
The eyes that fix you in a formulated phrase,
And when I am formulated, sprawling on a pin,
When I am pinned and wriggling on the wall,
Then how should I begin
To spit out all the butt-ends of my days and ways?
    And how should I presume?

    And I have known the arms already, known them all—
Arms that are braceleted and white and bare
(But in the lamplight, downed with light brown hair!)
Is it perfume from a dress
That makes me so digress?
Arms that lie along a table, or wrap about a shawl.
    And should I then presume?
    And how should I begin?
. . . . .
Shall I say, I have gone at dusk through narrow streets
And watched the smoke that rises from the pipes
Of lonely men in shirt-sleeves, leaning out of windows? . . .

  I should have been a pair of ragged claws
Scuttling across the floors of silent seas.

. . . . .

And the afternoon, the evening, sleeps so peacefully!
Smoothed by long fingers,
Asleep . . . tired . . . or it malingers,
Stretched on the floor, here beside you and me.
Should I, after tea and cakes and ices,
Have the strength to force the moment to its crisis?
But though I have wept and fasted, wept and prayed,
Though I have seen my head (grown slightly bald) brought in upon
    a platter,
I am no prophet—and here's no great matter;
I have seen the moment of my greatness flicker,
And I have seen the eternal Footman hold my coat, and snicker,
And in short, I was afraid.

  And would it have been worth it, after all,
After the cups, the marmalade, the tea,
Among the porcelain, among some talk of you and me,
Would it have been worth while,
To have bitten off the matter with a smile,
To have squeezed the universe into a ball
To roll it towards some overwhelming question,
To say: "I am Lazarus, come from the dead,
Come back to tell you all, I shall tell you all"—
If one, settling a pillow by her head,

Should say: "That is not what I meant at all.
That is not it, at all."

And would it have been worth it, after all,
Would it have been worth while,
After the sunsets and the dooryards and the sprinkled streets,
After the novels, after the teacups, after the skirts that trail along
    the floor—
And this, and so much more?—
It is impossible to say just what I mean!
But as if a magic lantern threw the nerves in patterns on a screen:
Would it have been worth while
If one, settling a pillow or throwing off a shawl,
And turning toward the window, should say:
    "That is not it at all,
    That is not what I meant, at all."
. . . . .
No! I am not Prince Hamlet, nor was meant to be;
Am an attendant lord, one that will do
To swell a progress, start a scene or two,
Advise the prince; no doubt, an easy tool,
Deferential, glad to be of use,
Politic, cautious, and meticulous;
Full of high sentence, but a bit obtuse;
At times, indeed, almost ridiculous—
Almost, at times, the Fool.

I grow old . . . I grow old . . .
I shall wear the bottoms of my trousers rolled.

Shall I part my hair behind? Do I dare to eat a peach?
I shall wear white flannel trousers, and walk upon the beach.
I have heard the mermaids singing, each to each.

I do not think that they will sing to me.

I have seen them riding seaward on the waves
Combing the white hair of the waves blown back
When the wind blows the water white and black.

We have lingered in the chambers of the sea
By sea-girls wreathed with seaweed red and brown
Till human voices wake us, and we drown.

ODYSSEUS ELYTIS

Translated from the Greek by Edmund Keeley and Philip Sherrard

The Mad Pomegranate Tree

Inquisitive matinal high spirits
à perdre haleine

In these all-white courtyards where the south wind blows
Whistling through vaulted arcades, tell me, is it the mad pome-
    granate tree
That leaps in the light, scattering its fruitful laughter
With windy wilfulness and whispering, tell me, is it the mad pome-
    granate tree
That quivers with foliage newly born at dawn
Raising high its colours in a shiver of triumph?

On plains where the naked girls awake,
When they harvest clover with their light brown arms
Roaming round the borders of their dreams—tell me, is it the mad
    pomegranate tree,
Unsuspecting, that puts the lights in their verdant baskets
That floods their names with the singing of birds—tell me
Is it the mad pomegranate tree that combats the cloudy skies of
    the world?

On the day that it adorns itself in jealousy with seven kinds of
    feathers,
Girding the eternal sun with a thousand blinding prisms
Tell me, is it the mad pomegranate tree
That seizes on the run a horse's mane of a hundred lashes,
Never sad and never grumbling—tell me, is it the mad pomegran-
    ate tree
That cries out the new hope now dawning?
Tell me, is that the mad pomegranate tree waving in the distance,
Fluttering a handkerchief of leaves of cool flame,
A sea near birth with a thousand ships and more,

With waves that a thousand times and more set out and go
To unscented shores—tell me, is it the mad pomegranate tree
That creaks the rigging aloft in the lucid air?

High as can be, with the blue bunch of grapes that flares and
    celebrates
Arrogant, full of danger—tell me, is it the mad pomegranate tree
That shatters with light the demon's tempests in the middle of the
    world
That spreads far as can be the saffron ruffle of day
Richly embroidered with scattered songs—tell me, is it the mad
    pomegranate tree
That hastily unfastens the silk apparel of day?

In petticoats of April first and cicadas of the feast of mid-August
Tell me, that which plays, that which rages, that which can entice
Shaking out of threats their evil black darkness
Spilling in the sun's embrace intoxicating birds
Tell me, that which opens its wings on the breast of things
On the breast of our deepest dreams, is that the mad pomegranate
    tree?

ROBERT FROST

An Old Man's Winter Night

All out-of-doors looked darkly in at him
Through the thin frost, almost in separate stars,
That gathers on the pane in empty rooms.
What kept his eyes from giving back the gaze
Was the lamp tilted near them in his hand.
What kept him from remembering what it was
That brought him to that creaking room was age.
He stood with barrels round him—at a loss.
And having scared the cellar under him
In clomping here, he scared it once again
In clomping off;—and scared the outer night,
Which has its sounds, familiar, like the roar
Of trees and crack of branches, common things,
But nothing so like beating on a box.
A light he was to no one but himself
Where now he sat, concerned with he knew what,
A quiet light, and then not even that.
He consigned to the moon, such as she was,
So late-arising, to the broken moon
As better than the sun in any case
For such a charge, his snow upon the roof,
His icicles along the wall to keep;
And slept. The log that shifted with a jolt
Once in the stove, disturbed him and he shifted,
And eased his heavy breathing, but still slept.
One aged man—one man—can't keep a house,
A farm, a countryside, or if he can,
It's thus he does it of a winter night.

G L O R I A   F U E R T E S
Translated from the Spanish by John Haines

Prayer

You are here on earth, our Father,
for I see you in the pine needle,
in the blue torso of the worker,
in the small girl who embroiders
with bent shoulder, mixing the thread on her finger.
Our Father here on earth,
in the furrow,
in the orchard,
in the mine,
in the seaport,
in the movie house,
in the wine,
in the house of the doctor.
Our Father here on earth,
where you have your glory and your hell,
and your limbo in the cafés
where the rich have their cool drink.
Our Father who sits in school without paying,
you are in the groceryman,
and in the man who is hungry,
and in the poet—never in the usurer!
Our Father here on earth,
reading on a bench of the Prado,
you are the old man feeding breadcrumbs to the birds on the walk.
Our Father here on earth,
in the cigarette, in the kiss,
in the grain of wheat, in the hearts
of all those who are good.
Father who can live anywhere,

God who moves into any loneliness,
you who quiet our anguish, here on earth,
Our Father, yes we see you,
those of us who will see you soon,
wherever you are, or there in heaven.

ALLEN GINSBERG

A Supermarket in California

What thoughts I have of you tonight, Walt Whitman, for I walked down the sidestreets under the trees with a headache self-conscious looking at the full moon.

In my hungry fatigue, and shopping for images, I went into the neon fruit supermarket, dreaming of your enumerations!

What peaches and what penumbras! Whole families shopping at night! Aisles full of husbands! Wives in the avocados, babies in the tomatoes!—and you, García Lorca, what were you doing down by the watermelons?

I saw you, Walt Whitman, childless, lonely old grubber, poking among the meats in the refrigerator and eyeing the grocery boys.

I heard you asking questions of each: Who killed the pork chops? What price bananas? Are you my Angel?

I wandered in and out of the brilliant stacks of cans following you, and followed in my imagination by the store detective.

We strode down the open corridors together in our solitary fancy tasting artichokes, possessing every frozen delicacy, and never passing the cashier.

Where are we going, Walt Whitman? The doors close in an hour. Which way does your beard point tonight?

(I touch your book and dream of our odyssey in the supermarket and feel absurd.)

Will we walk all night through solitary streets? The trees add shade to shade, lights out in the houses, we'll both be lonely.

Will we stroll dreaming of the lost America of love past blue automobiles in driveways, home to our silent cottage?

Ah, dear father, graybeard, lonely old courage-teacher, what America did you have when Charon quit poling his ferry and you got out on a smoking bank and stood watching the boat disappear on the black waters of Lethe?

Lament

Your dying was a difficult enterprise.
First, petty things took up your energies,
The small but clustering duties of the sick,
Irritant as the cough's dry rhetoric.
Those hours of waiting for pills, shot, X-ray
Or test (while you read novels two a day)
Already with a kind of clumsy stealth
Distanced you from the habits of your health.
  In hope still, courteous still, but tired and thin,
You tried to stay the man that you had been,
Treating each symptom as a mere mishap
Without import. But then the spinal tap.
It brought a hard headache, and when night came
I heard you wake up from the same bad dream
Every half-hour with the same short cry
Of mild outrage, before immediately
Slipping into the nightmare once again
Empty of content but the drip of pain.
No respite followed: though the nightmare ceased,
Your cough grew thick and rich, its strength increased.
Four nights, and on the fifth we drove you down
To the Emergency Room. That frown, that frown:
I'd never seen such rage in you before
As when they wheeled you through the swinging door.
For you knew, rightly, they conveyed you from
Those normal pleasures of the sun's kingdom
The hedonistic body basks within
And takes for granted—summer on the skin,
Sleep without break, the moderate taste of tea

In a dry mouth. You had gone on from me
As if your body sought out martyrdom
In the far Canada of a hospital room.
Once there, you entered fully the distress
And long pale rigours of the wilderness.
A gust of morphine hid you. Back in sight
You breathed through a segmented tube, fat, white,
Jammed down your throat so that you could not speak.
   How thin the distance made you. In your cheek
One day, appeared the true shape of your bone
No longer padded. Still your mind, alone,
Explored this emptying intermediate
State for what holds and rests were hidden in it.
   You wrote us messages on a pad, amused
At one time that you had your nurse confused
Who, seeing you reconciled after four years
With your grey father, both of you in tears,
Asked if this was at last your 'special friend'
(The one you waited for until the end).
"She sings," you wrote, "a Philippine folk song
To wake me in the morning . . . It is long
And very pretty." Grabbing at detail
To furnish this bare ledge toured by the gale,
On which you lay, bed restful as a knife,
You tried, tried hard, to make of it a life
Thick with the complicating circumstance
Your thoughts might fasten on. It had been chance
Always till now that had filled up the moment

With live specifics your hilarious comment
Discovered as it went along; and fed,
Laconic, quick, wherever it was led.
You improvised upon your own delight.
I think back to the scented summer night
We talked between our sleeping bags, below
A molten field of stars five years ago:
I was so tickled by your mind's light touch
I couldn't sleep, you made me laugh too much,
Though I was tired and begged you to leave off.

Now you were tired, and yet not tired enough
—Still hungry for the great world you were losing
Steadily in no season of your choosing—
And when at last the whole death was assured,
Drugs having failed, and when you had endured
Two weeks of an abominable constraint,
You faced it equably, without complaint,
Unwhimpering, but not at peace with it.
You'd lived as if your time was infinite:
You were not ready and not reconciled,
Feeling as uncompleted as a child
Till you had shown the world what you could do
In some ambitious role to be worked through,
A role your need for it had half-defined,
But never wholly, even in your mind.
You lacked the necessary ruthlessness,
The soaring meanness that pinpoints success.

We loved that lack of self-love, and your smile,
Rueful, at your own silliness.
                              Meanwhile,
Your lungs collapsed, and the machine, unstrained,
Did all your breathing now. Nothing remained
But death by drowning on an inland sea
Of your own fluids, which it seemed could be
Kindly forestalled by drugs. Both could and would:
Nothing was said, everything understood,
At least by us. Your own concerns were not
Long-term, precisely, when they gave the shot
—You made local arrangements to the bed
And pulled a pillow round beside your head.
    And so you slept, and died, your skin gone grey,
Achieving your completeness, in a way.

Outdoors next day, I was dizzy from a sense
Of being ejected with some violence
From vigil in a white and distant spot
Where I was numb, into this garden plot
Too warm, too close, and not enough like pain.
I was delivered into time again
—The variations that I live among
Where your long body too used to belong
And where the still bush is minutely active.
You never thought your body was attractive,
Though others did, and yet you trusted it
And must have loved its fickleness a bit
Since it was yours and gave you what it could,

Till near the end it let you down for good,
Its blood hospitable to those guests who
Took over by betraying it into
The greatest of its inconsistencies
This difficult, tedious, painful enterprise.

T H O M A S   H A R D Y
(Lines on the loss of the "Titanic")

The Convergence of the Twain

I

In a solitude of the sea
Deep from human vanity,
And the Pride of Life that planned her, stilly couches she.

II

Steel chambers, late the pyres
Of her salamandrine fires,
Cold currents thrid, and turn to rhythmic tidal lyres.

III

Over the mirrors meant
To glass the opulent
The sea-worm crawls—grotesque, slimed, dumb, indifferent.

IV

Jewels in joy designed
To ravish the sensuous mind
Lie lightless, all their sparkles bleared and black and blind.

V

Dim moon-eyed fishes near
  Gaze at the gilded gear
And query: "What does this vaingloriousness down here?"

VI

Well: while was fashioning
  This creature of cleaving wing;
The Immanent Will that stirs and urges everything

VII

Prepared a sinister mate
  For her—so gaily great
A Shape of Ice, for the time far and dissociate.

VIII

And as the smart ship grew
  In stature, grace, and hue,
In shadowy silent distance grew the Iceberg too.

IX

Alien they seemed to be;
No mortal eye could see
The intimate welding of their later history,

X

Or sign that they were bent
By paths coincident
On being anon twin halves of one august event,

XI

Till the Spinner of the Years
Said "Now!" And each one hears,
And consummation comes, and jars two hemispheres.

GWEN HARWOOD

At Mornington

They told me that when I was taken
to the sea's edge, for the first time,
I leapt from my father's arms
and was caught by a wave and rolled
like a doll among rattling shells;
and I seem to remember my father
fully clothed, still streaming with water,
half comforting, half angry.
And indeed I remember believing
as a child, I could walk on water—
the next wave, the next wave—
it was only a matter of balance.

On what flood are they borne,
these memories of early childhood,
iridescent, fugitive
as light in a sea-wet shell,
while we stand, two friends of middle age,
by your parents' grave in silence
among avenues of the dead
with their cadences of trees,
marble and granite parting
the quick of autumn grasses.
We have the wholeness of this day
to share as we will between us.

This morning I saw in your garden
fine pumpkins grown on a trellis
so it seemed that the vines were rising

to flourish the fruits of earth
above their humble station
in airy defiance of nature
—a parable of myself,
a skinful of elements climbing
from earth to the fastness of light;
now come to that time of life
when our bones begin to wear us,
to settle our flesh in final shape

as the drying face of land
rose out of earth's seamless waters.
   I dreamed once, long ago,
   that we walked among day-bright flowers
   to a bench in the Brisbane gardens
   with a pitcher of water between us,
   and stayed for a whole day
   talking, and drinking the water.
   Then, as night fell, you said
   "There is still some water left over."
We have one day, only one,
but more than enough to refresh us.

At your side among the graves
I think of death no more
than when, secure in my father's arms,
I laughed at a hollowed pumpkin
with candle flame for eyesight,
and when I am seized at last

and rolled in one grinding race
of dreams, pain, memories, love and grief,
from which no hand will save me,
the peace of this day will shine
like light on the face of the waters
that bear me away for ever.

Witch Doctor

I

He dines alone surrounded by reflections
of himself. Then after sleep and benzedrine
descends the Cinquecento stair his magic
wrought from hypochondria of the well-
to-do and nagging deathwish of the poor;
swirls on smiling genuflections of
his liveried chauffeur into a crested
lilac limousine, the cynosure
of mousey neighbors tittering behind
Venetian blinds and half afraid of him
and half admiring his outrageous flair.

II

Meanwhile his mother, priestess in gold lamé,
precedes him to the quondam theater
now Israel Temple of the Highest Alpha,
where the bored, the sick, the alien, the tired
await euphoria. With deadly vigor
she prepares the way for mystery
and lucre. Shouts in blues-contralto, "He's
God's dictaphone of all-redeeming truth.
Oh he's the holyweight champeen who's come
to give the knockout lick to your bad luck;
say he's the holyweight champeen who's here
to deal a knockout punch to your hard luck."

III

Reposing on cushions of black leopard skin,
he telephones instructions for a long
slow drive across the park that burgeons now
with spring and sailors. Peers questingly
into the green fountainous twilight, sighs
and turns the gold-plate dial to Music For
Your Dining-Dancing Pleasure. Smoking Egyptian
cigarettes rehearses in his mind
a new device that he must use tonight.

IV

Approaching Israel Temple, mask in place,
he hears ragtime allegros of a "Song
of Zion" that becomes when he appears
a hallelujah wave for him to walk.
His mother and a rainbow-surpliced cordon
conduct him choiring to the altar-stage,
and there he kneels and seems to pray before
a lighted Jesus painted sealskin-brown.
Then with a glittering flourish he arises,
turns, gracefully extends his draperied arms:
"Israelites, true Jews, O found lost tribe
of Israel, receive my blessing now.
Selah, selah." He feels them yearn toward him
as toward a lover, exults before the image

of himself their trust gives back. Stands as though
in meditation, letting their eyes caress
his garments jewelled and chatoyant, cut
to fall, to flow from his tall figure
dramatically just so. Then all at once
he sways, quivers, gesticulates as if
to ward off blows or kisses, and when he speaks
again he utters wildering vocables,
hypnotic no-words planned (and never failing)
to enmesh his flock in theopathic tension.
Cries of eudaemonic pain attest
his artistry. Behind the mask he smiles.
And now in subtly altering light he chants
and sinuously trembles, chants and trembles
while convulsive energies of eager faith
surcharge the theater with power of
their own, a power he has counted on
and for a space allows to carry him.
Dishevelled antiphons proclaim the moment
his followers all day have hungered for,
but which is his alone.

He signals: tambourines begin, frenetic
drumbeat and glissando. He dances from the altar,
robes hissing, flaring, shimmering; down aisles
where mantled guardsmen intercept wild hands
that arduously strain to clutch his vestments,
he dances, dances, ensorcelled and aloof,
the fervid juba of God as lover, healer,
conjurer. And of himself as God.

ANTHONY HECHT

"More Light! More Light!"

for Heinrich Blücher and Hannah Arendt

Composed in the Tower before his execution
These moving verses, and being brought at that time
Painfully to the stake, submitted, declaring thus:
"I implore my God to witness that I have made no crime."

Nor was he forsaken of courage, but the death was horrible,
The sack of gunpowder failing to ignite.
His legs were blistered sticks on which the black sap
Bubbled and burst as he howled for the Kindly Light.

And that was but one, and by no means one of the worst;
Permitted at least his pitiful dignity;
And such as were by made prayers in the name of Christ,
That shall judge all men, for his soul's tranquillity.

We move now to outside a German wood.
Three men are there commanded to dig a hole
In which the two Jews are ordered to lie down
And be buried alive by the third, who is a Pole.

Not light from the shrine at Weimar beyond the hill
Nor light from heaven appeared. But he did refuse.
A Lüger settled back deeply in its glove.
He was ordered to change places with the Jews.

Much casual death had drained away their souls.
The thick dirt mounted toward the quivering chin.
When only the head was exposed the order came
To dig him out again and to get back in.

No light, no light in the blue Polish eye.
When he finished a riding boot packed down the earth.
The Lüger hovered lightly in its glove.
He was shot in the belly and in three hours bled to death.

No prayers or incense rose up in those hours
Which grew to be years, and every day came mute
Ghosts from the ovens, sifting through crisp air,
And settled upon his eyes in a black soot.

ZBIGNIEW HERBERT

Translated from the Polish by John Carpenter and Bogdana Carpenter

Mr. Cogito Thinks About Hell

The lowest circle of hell. Contrary to prevailing opinion it is inhabited neither by despots nor matricides, nor even by those who go after the bodies of others. It is the refuge of artists, full of mirrors, musical instruments, and pictures. At first glance this is the most luxurious infernal department, without tar, fire, or physical tortures.

Throughout the year competitions, festivals, and concerts are held here. There is no climax in the season. The climax is permanent and almost absolute. Every few months new trends come into being and nothing, it appears, is capable of stopping the triumphant march of the avant-garde.

Beelzebub loves art. He boasts that already his choruses, his poets, and his painters are nearly superior to those of heaven. He who has better art has better government—that's clear. Soon they will be able to measure their strength against one another at the Festival of the Two Worlds. And then we will see what remains of Dante, Fra Angelico, and Bach.

Beelzebub supports the arts. He provides his artists with calm, good board, and absolute isolation from hellish life.

NAZIM HIKMET

Translated from the Turkish by Randy Blasing and Mutlu Konuk

Things I Didn't Know I Loved

it's 1962 March 28th
I'm sitting by the window on the Prague-Berlin train
night is falling
I never knew I liked
night descending like a tired bird on a smoky wet plain
I don't like
comparing nightfall to a tired bird

I didn't know I loved the earth
can someone who hasn't worked the earth love it
I've never worked the earth
it must be my only Platonic love

and here I've loved rivers all this time
whether motionless like this they curl skirting the hills
European hills crowned with chateaus
or whether stretched out flat as far as the eye can see
I know you can't wash in the same river even once
I know the river will bring new lights you'll never see
I know we live slightly longer than a horse but not nearly as long
   as a crow
I know this has troubled people before
                and will trouble those after me
I know all this has been said a thousand times before
                and will be said after me

I didn't know I loved the sky
cloudy or clear
the blue vault Andrei studied on his back at Borodino

in prison I translated both volumes of *War and Peace* into Turkish
I hear voices
not from the blue vault but from the yard
the guards are beating someone again

I didn't know I loved trees
bare beeches near Moscow in Peredelkino
they come upon me in winter noble and modest
beeches are Russian the way poplars are Turkish
"the poplars of Izmir
losing their leaves . . .
they call me The Knife . . .
                              lover like a young tree . . .
I blow stately mansions sky-high"
in the Ilgaz woods in 1920 I tied an embroidered linen handkerchief
                              to a pine bough for luck

I never knew I loved roads
even the asphalt kind
Vera's behind the wheel we're driving from Moscow to the Crimea
                              Koktebele
                    formerly "Goktepé ili" in Turkish
the two of us inside a closed box
the world flows past on both sides distant and mute
I was never so close to anyone in my life
bandits stopped me on the red road between Bolu and Geredé
                              when I was eighteen
apart from my life I didn't have anything in the wagon they
    could take

and at eighteen our lives are what we value least
I've written this somewhere before
wading through a dark muddy street I'm going to the shadow play
Ramazan night
a paper lantern leading the way
maybe nothing like this ever happened
maybe I read it somewhere an eight-year-old boy
                                     going to the shadow play
Ramazan night in Istanbul holding his grandfather's hand
    his grandfather has on a fez and is wearing the fur coat
        with a sable collar over his robe
     and there's a lantern in the servant's hand
     and I can't contain myself for joy

flowers come to mind for some reason
poppies cactuses jonquils
in the jonquil garden in Kadikoy Istanbul I kissed Marika
fresh almonds on her breath
I was seventeen
my heart on a swing touched the sky
I didn't know I loved flowers
friends sent me three red carnations in prison

I just remembered the stars
I love them too
whether I'm floored watching them from below
or whether I'm flying at their side

I have some questions for the cosmonauts
were the stars much bigger
did they look like huge jewels on black velvet
                              or apricots on òrange
did you feel proud to get closer to the stars
I saw color photos of the cosmos in *Ogonek* magazine now don't
        be upset comrades but nonfigurative shall we say or abstract
        well some of them looked just like such paintings which is to
        say they were terribly figurative and concrete
my heart was in my mouth looking at them
they are our endless desire to grasp things
seeing them I could even think of death and not feel at all sad
I never knew I loved the cosmos

snow flashes in front of my eyes
both heavy wet steady snow and the dry whirling kind
I didn't know I liked snow

I never knew I loved the sun
even when setting cherry-red as now
in Istanbul too it sometimes sets in postcard colors
but you aren't about to paint it that way
I didn't know I loved the sea
                        except the Sea of Azov
or how much

I didn't know I loved clouds
whether I'm under or up above them
whether they look like giants or shaggy white beasts

moonlight the falsest the most languid the most petit-bourgeois
strikes me
I like it

I didn't know I liked rain
whether it falls like a fine net or splatters against the glass my
      heart leaves me tangled up in a net or trapped inside a drop
      and takes off for uncharted countries I didn't know I loved
      rain but why did I suddenly discover all these passions sitting
      by the window on the Prague-Berlin train
is it because I lit my sixth cigarette
one alone could kill me
is it because I'm half dead from thinking about someone back in
   Moscow
her hair straw-blond eyelashes blue

the train plunges on through the pitch-black night
I never knew I liked the night pitch-black
sparks fly from the engine
I didn't know I loved sparks
I didn't know I loved so many things and I had to wait until sixty
      to find it out sitting by the window on the Prague-Berlin train
      watching the world disappear as if on a journey of no return

MAX JACOB
Translated from the French by John Ashbery

Translated from the German or the Bosnian

To Madame Edouard Fillacier

My horse is halting! Halt thine own as well, comrade, I am afraid! Between the slopes of the hill and us, the swarded slopes of the hill, there is a woman, unless it be a great cloud. Halt! She calls me! She calls me and I see her palpitating breast! Her arms signal me to follow her, her arm . . . unless her arm be a cloud.

Halt, comrade, I am afraid, halt! Between the trees of the hill, the slanting trees of the hill, I saw an eye, if that eye be not a cloud. It gazes at me, it troubles me: halt! It follows in our tracks on the high road, if that eye be not a cloud.

Listen, comrade! phantoms, lives of this earth or of another, let us not speak of these beings in the town lest they call us nuisances.

FRANCIS JAMMES
Translated from the French by Richard Wilbur

A Prayer to Go to Paradise with the Donkeys

to Máire and Jack

When I must come to you, O my God, I pray
It be some dusty-roaded holiday,
And even as in my travels here below,
I beg to choose by what road I shall go
To Paradise, where the clear stars shine by day.
I'll take my walking-stick and go my way,
And to my friends the donkeys I shall say,
"I am Francis Jammes, and I'm going to Paradise,
For there is no hell in the land of the loving God."
And I'll say to them: "Come, sweet friends of the blue skies,
Poor creatures who with a flap of the ears or a nod
Of the head shake off the buffets, the bees, the flies . . ."

Let me come with these donkeys, Lord, into your land,
These beasts who bow their heads so gently, and stand
With their small feet joined together in a fashion
Utterly gentle, asking your compassion.
I shall arrive, followed by their thousands of ears,
Followed by those with baskets at their flanks,
By those who lug the carts of mountebanks
Or loads of feather-dusters and kitchen-wares,
By those with humps of battered water-cans,
By bottle-shaped she-asses who halt and stumble,
By those tricked out in little pantaloons
To cover their wet, blue galls where flies assemble
In whirling swarms, making a drunken hum.
Dear God, let it be with these donkeys that I come,
And let it be that angels lead us in peace
To leafy streams where cherries tremble in air,

Sleek as the laughing flesh of girls; and there
In that haven of souls let it be that, leaning above
Your divine waters, I shall resemble these donkeys,
Whose humble and sweet poverty will appear
Clear in the clearness of your eternal love.

ROBINSON JEFFERS

The Deer Lay Down Their Bones

I followed the narrow cliffside trail half way up the mountain
Above the deep river-canyon. There was a little cataract crossed
    the path, flinging itself
Over tree roots and rocks, shaking the jeweled fern-fronds, bright
    bubbling water
Pure from the mountain, but a bad smell came up. Wondering at it
    I clambered down the steep stream.
Some forty feet, and found in the midst of bush-oak and laurel,
Hung like a bird's nest on the precipice brink a small hidden clear-
    ing,
Grass and a shallow pool. But all about there were bones lying in
    the grass, clean bones and stinking bones,
Antlers and bones: I understood that the place was a refuge for
    wounded deer; there are so many
Hurt ones escape the hunters and limp away to lie hidden; here
    they have water for the awful thirst
And peace to die in; dense green laurel and grim cliff
Make sanctuary, and a sweet wind blows upward from the deep
    gorge.—I wish my bones were with theirs.
But that's a foolish thing to confess, and a little cowardly. We know
    that life
Is on the whole quite equally good and bad, mostly gray neutral,
    and can be endured
To the dim end, no matter what magic of grass, water and
    precipice, and pain of wounds,
Makes death look dear. We have been given life and have used it—
    not a great gift perhaps—but in honesty
Should use it all. Mine's empty since my love died—Empty? The
    flame-haired grandchild with great blue eyes

That look like hers?—What can I do for the child? I gaze at her
and wonder what sort of man
In the fall of the world . . . I am growing old, that is the trouble.
My children and little grandchildren
Will find their way, and why should I wait ten years yet, having
lived sixty-seven, ten years more or less,
Before I crawl out on a ledge of rock and die snapping, like a wolf
Who has lost his mate?—I am bound by my own thirty-year-old
decision: who drinks the wine
Should take the dregs; even in the bitter lees and sediment
New discovery may lie. The deer in that beautiful place lay down
their bones: I must wear mine.

ROBERTO JUARROZ

Translated from the French by W. S. Merwin

Life draws a tree
and death draws another one.
Life draws a nest
and death copies it.
Life draws a bird
to live in the nest
and right away death
draws another bird.

A hand that draws nothing
wanders among the drawings
and at times moves one of them.
For example:
a bird of life
occupies death's nest
on the tree that life drew.

Other times
the hand that draws nothing
blots out one drawing of the series.
For example:
the tree of death
holds the nest of death,
but there's no bird in it.

And other times
the hand that draws nothing
itself changes
into an extra image

in the shape of a bird,
in the shape of a tree,
in the shape of a nest.
And then, only then,
nothing's missing and nothing's left over.
For example:
two birds
occupy life's nest
in death's tree.

Or life's tree
holds two nests
with only one bird in them.

Or a single bird
lives in the one nest
on the tree of life
and the tree of death.

Psalm and Lament

Hialeah, Florida

The clocks are sorry, the clocks are very sad.
One stops, one goes on striking the wrong hours.

And the grass burns terribly in the sun,
The grass turns yellow secretly at the roots.

Now suddenly the yard chairs look empty, the sky looks empty,
The sky looks vast and empty.

Out on Red Road the traffic continues; everything continues.
Nor does memory sleep; it goes on.

Out spring the butterflies of recollection,
And I think that for the first time I understand

The beautiful ordinary light of this patio
And even perhaps the dark rich earth of a heart.

(The bedclothes, they say, had been pulled down.
I will not describe it. I do not want to describe it.

No, but the sheets were drenched and twisted.
They were the very handkerchiefs of grief.)

Let summer come now with its schoolboy trumpets and fountains.
But the years are gone, the years are finally over.

And there is only
This long desolation of flower-bordered sidewalks

That runs to the corner, turns, and goes on,
That disappears and goes on

Into the black oblivion of a neighborhood and a world
Without billboards or yesterdays.

Sometimes a sad moon comes and waters the roof tiles.
But the years are gone. There are no more years.

in memory of my mother (1897–1974)

One Train May Hide Another

(sign at a railroad crossing in Kenya)

In a poem, one line may hide another line,
As at a crossing, one train may hide another train.
That is, if you are waiting to cross
The tracks, wait to do it for one moment at
Least after the first train is gone. And so when you read
Wait until you have read the next line—
Then it is safe to go on reading.
In a family one sister may conceal another,
So, when you are courting, it's best to have them all in view
Otherwise in coming to find one you may love another.
One father or one brother may hide the man,
If you are a woman, whom you have been waiting to love.
So always standing in front of something the other
As words stand in front of objects, feelings, and ideas.
One wish may hide another. And one person's reputation may hide
The reputation of another. One dog may conceal another
On a lawn, so if you escape the first one you're not necessarily safe;
One lilac may hide another and then a lot of lilacs and on the
   Appia Antica one tomb
May hide a number of other tombs. In love, one reproach may
   hide another,
One small complaint may hide a great one.
One injustice may hide another—one colonial may hide another,
One blaring red uniform another, and another, a whole column.
   One bath may hide another bath
As when, after bathing, one walks out into the rain.
One idea may hide another: Life is simple
Hide Life is incredibly complex, as in the prose of Gertrude Stein

One sentence hides another and is another as well. And in the
   laboratory
One invention may hide another invention,
One evening may hide another, one shadow, a nest of shadows.
One dark red, or one blue, or one purple—this is a painting
By someone after Matisse. One waits at the tracks until they pass,
These hidden doubles or, sometimes, likenesses. One identical
   twin
May hide the other. And there may be even more in there! The
   obstetrician
Gazes at the Valley of the Var. We used to live there, my wife and
   I, but
One life hid another life. And now she is gone and I am here.
A vivacious mother hides a gawky daughter. The daughter hides
Her own vivacious daughter in turn. They are in
A railway station and the daughter is holding a bag
Bigger than her mother's bag and successfully hides it.
In offering to pick up the daughter's bag one finds oneself con-
   fronted by the mother's
And has to carry that one, too. So one hitchhiker
May deliberately hide another and one cup of coffee
Another, too, until one is over-excited. One love may hide another
   love or the same love
As when "I love you" suddenly rings false and one discovers
The better love lingering behind, as when "I'm full of doubts"
Hides "I'm certain about something and it is that"
And one dream may hide another as is well known, always, too. In
   the Garden of Eden
Adam and Eve may hide the real Adam and Eve.

Jerusalem may hide another Jerusalem.
When you come to something, stop to let it pass
So you can see what else is there. At home, no matter where,
Internal tracks pose dangers, too: one memory
Certainly hides another, that being what memory is all about,
The eternal reverse succession of contemplated entities. Reading
    A Sentimental Journey look around
When you have finished, for *Tristram Shandy*, to see
If it is standing there, it should be, stronger
And more profound and theretofore hidden as Santa Maria
    Maggiore
May be hidden by similar churches inside Rome. One sidewalk
May hide another, as when you're asleep there, and
One song hide another song; a pounding upstairs
Hide the beating of drums. One friend may hide another, you sit at
    the foot of a tree
With one and when you get up to leave there is another
Whom you'd have preferred to talk to all along. One teacher,
One doctor, one ecstasy, one illness, one woman, one man
May hide another. Pause to let the first one pass.
You think, Now it is safe to cross and you are hit by the next one.
    It can be important
To have waited at least a moment to see what was already there.

Next, Please

Always too eager for the future, we
Pick up bad habits of expectancy.
Something is always approaching; every day
Till then we say,

Watching from a bluff the tiny, clear,
Sparkling armada of promises draw near.
How slow they are! And how much time they waste,
Refusing to make haste!

Yet still they leave us holding wretched stalks
Of disappointment, for, though nothing balks
Each big approach, leaning with brasswork prinked,
Each rope distinct,

Flagged, and the figurehead with golden tits
Arching our way, it never anchors; it's
No sooner present than it turns to past.
Right to the last

We think each one will heave to and unload
All good into our lives, all we are owed
For waiting so devoutly and so long.
But we are wrong:

Only one ship is seeking us, a black-
Sailed unfamiliar, towing at her back
A huge and birdless silence. In her wake
No waters breed or break.

D . H . L A W R E N C E

The Ship of Death

I

Now it is autumn and the falling fruit
and the long journey towards oblivion.

The apples falling like great drops of dew
to bruise themselves an exit from themselves.

And it is time to go, to bid farewell
to one's own self, and find an exit
from the fallen self.

II

Have you built your ship of death, O have you?
O build your ship of death, for you will need it.

The grim frost is at hand, when the apples will fall
thick, almost thundrous, on the hardened earth.

And death is on the air like a smell of ashes!
Ah! can't you smell it?

And in the bruised body, the frightened soul
finds itself shrinking, wincing from the cold
that blows upon it through the orifices.

III

And can a man his own quietus make
with a bare bodkin?

With daggers, bodkins, bullets, man can make
a bruise or break of exit for his life;
but is that a quietus, O tell me, is it quietus?

Surely not so! for how could murder, even self-murder
ever a quietus make?

IV

O let us talk of quiet that we know,
that we can know, the deep and lovely quiet
of a strong heart at peace!

How can we this, our own quietus, make?

V

Build then the ship of death, for you must take
the longest journey, to oblivion.

And die the death, the long and painful death
that lies between the old self and the new.

Already our bodies are fallen, bruised, badly bruised,
already our souls are oozing through the exit
of the cruel bruise.

Already the dark and endless ocean of the end
is washing in through the breaches of our wounds,
already the flood is upon us.

Oh build your ship of death, your little ark
and furnish it with food, with little cakes, and wine
for the dark flight down oblivion.

        VI

Piecemeal the body dies, and the timid soul
has her footing washed away, as the dark flood rises.

We are dying, we are dying, we are all of us dying
and nothing will stay the death-flood rising within us
and soon it will rise on the world, on the outside world.

We are dying, we are dying, piecemeal our bodies are dying
and our strength leaves us,
and our soul cowers naked in the dark rain over the flood,
cowering in the last branches of the tree of our life.

VII

We are dying, we are dying, so all we can do
is now to be willing to die, and to build the ship
of death to carry the soul on the longest journey.

A little ship, with oars and food
and little dishes, and all accoutrements
fitting and ready for the departing soul.

Now launch the small ship, now as the body dies
and life departs, launch out, the fragile soul
in the fragile ship of courage, the ark of faith
with its store of food and little cooking pans
and change of clothes,
upon the flood's black waste
upon the waters of the end
upon the sea of death, where still we sail
darkly, for we cannot steer, and have no port.

There is no port, there is nowhere to go
only the deepening black darkening still-
blacker upon the soundless, ungurgling flood
darkness at one with darkness, up and down
and sideways utterly dark, so there is no direction any more.
And the little ship is there; yet she is gone.

She is not seen, for there is nothing to see her by.
She is gone! gone! and yet
somewhere she is there.
Nowhere!

VIII

And everything is gone, the body is gone
completely under, gone, entirely gone.
The upper darkness is heavy on the lower,
between them the little ship
is gone
she is gone.

It is the end, it is oblivion.

IX

And yet out of eternity, a thread
separates itself on the blackness,
a horizontal thread
that fumes a little with pallor upon the dark.
Is it illusion? or does the pallor fume
A little higher?

Ah wait, wait, for there's the dawn,
the cruel dawn of coming back to life
out of oblivion.

Wait, wait, the little ship
drifting, beneath the deathly ashy grey
of a flood-dawn.

Wait, wait! even so, a flush of yellow
and strangely, O chilled wan soul, a flush of rose.

A flush of rose, and the whole thing starts again.

     X

The flood subsides, and the body, like a worn sea-shell
emerges strange and lovely.
And the little ship wings home, faltering and lapsing
on the pink flood,
and the frail soul steps out, into her house again
filling the heart with peace.

Swings the heart renewed with peace
even of oblivion.

Oh build your ship of death, oh build it!
for you will need it.
For the voyage of oblivion awaits you.

ENRIQUE LIHN
Translated from the Spanish by David Unger

The Old Man's Monologue with Death

And so, that was all of it.
Your life is before you, look at yourself in it as you would in a mirror,
cloud it up with your last breath.
That's you as a boy, among others your age:
would you recognize yourself on sight?
They've hit you in the face, you're crying openly,
they've hit you in the face.

There you are a few years later with your grandfather
facing the first corpse you've ever seen.
You cry for the old man, it seems you cry for him
but it's really because you fear the unknown.
A fly circling in the air distracts you.

And now your sins appear, the few pleasures of a body reduced to
    its least expression,
a fifteen-year-old made of wretched flesh;
and your virtues also appear, struggling with gestures
that are even emptier than themselves.
A great love, the pearl of your neighborhood,
cheerfully steals your heart
to play with it at the end of a string.
To the seminary now,
they've hit you in the face. You turn the other cheek;
but God doesn't last very long, times have changed
and you're caught committing a sacrilege.
Look at yourself in that situation, that was all:
Killing a dead man who shouts at you: I don't exist.
Marx and the devil exist.

Think back, that's you at thirty;
you haven't been able to marry
your woman, the wife of another man.
You live in a basement, in a crypt
you take what's handed to you, without a job,
thin as a skeleton, just like a saint.
On certain nights, your father's father
comes to visit you from the other world:
"Retrace your steps my son, let go
of the red paradise that sucks out your blood.
Even if the world changes through violence,
the dead will be the first to die.
Think of yourself, set up a small business.
Charity begins at home."

Look a little closer, you are that man
patching up his only shirt
crying without passion in the shadows.
You're coming back from the station, someone has left,
but it wasn't love, only a sickly woman
getting on in years, without children, set on forgetting you
just at the moment of leaving.
You put yourself in her place. You don't suffer.
Was that love? Okay, so it was.
Relax. A woman getting older. Relax.
Take a closer look at her. Who was she? You don't even remember,
but it's she, the one who hates the holes in your socks,
the one who demands yet rejects a child,
who pretends to be sleeping when you get home,

who wakes you up to ask you where you've been,
who pokes fun at your old books,
who sarcastically serves you an empty plate,
who threatens to become a nun,
who finally disappears into a crowd.

Well, that was all of it. Look at yourself sitting,
an old man among others your age,
hunched over in a public square.
You shuffle your feet, an eye twitches,
the pigeons eating the bread crumbs at your feet
shun you though you're the one feeding them.
No one knows who you are, not even you recognize yourself
when you see your shadow.
Music that brings back no memories makes you cry.
You live off your forgetfulness
in the pit of an old house.
Well then, why not just die in peace?
What's this leading up to?
That's enough, close your eyes;
don't get upset, relax, enough is enough.
Enough, enough, easy now, here is death.

JORGE DE LIMA

Translated from the Portuguese by Dudley Poore

The Big Mystical Circus

Frederick Knieps, Physician of the Bed-Chamber to the Empress
   Theresa,
resolved that his son also should be a doctor,
but the youth, having established relations with Agnes, the
   tightrope artist,
married her and founded the circus dynasty of Knieps
with which the newspapers are so much concerned.
Charlotte, the daughter of Frederick, married the clown,
Whence sprang Marie and Otto.
Otto married Lily Braun, the celebrated contortionist,
who had a saint's image tattooed on her belly.
The daughter of Lily Braun—she of the tattooed belly—
wanted to enter a convent,
but Otto Frederick Knieps would not consent,
and Margaret continued the circus dynasty
with which the newspapers are so much concerned.
Then Margaret had her body tattooed,
suffering greatly for the love of God,
and caused to be engraved on her rosy skin
the Fourteen Stations of our Lord's Passion.
No tiger ever attacked her;
the lion Nero, who had already eaten two ventriloquists,
when she entered his cage nude,
wept like a new-born babe.
Her husband, the trapeze artist Ludwig, never could love her
   thereafter,
because the sacred engravings obliterated
both her skin and his desire.
Then the pugilist Rudolph, who was an atheist

and a cruel man, attacked Margaret and violated her.

After this, he was converted and died.

Margaret bore two daughters who are the wonder of Knieps' Great
    Circus.

But the greatest of miracles is their virginity,

against which bankers and gentlemen with monocles beat in vain;

their levitations, which the audience thinks a fraud;

their chastity, in which nobody believes;

their magic, which the simple-minded say is the devil's;

yet the children believe in them, are their faithful followers, their
    friends, their devoted worshipers.

Marie and Helène perform nude;

they dance on the wire and so dislocate their limbs

that their arms and legs no longer appear their own.

The spectators shout encore to thighs, encore to breasts, encore to
    armpits.

Marie and Helène give themselves wholly,

and are shared by cynical men;

but their souls, which nobody sees, they keep pure.

And when they display their limbs in the sight of men,

They display their souls in the sight of God.

With the true history of Knieps' Great Circus

the newspapers are very little concerned.

FEDERICO GARCÍA LORCA

Translated from the Spanish by Rolfe Humphries

The Unfaithful Married Woman

I took her to the river,
Believing her unwed;
The fact she had a husband
Was something left unsaid.
St. James's night is timely—
She would not let me wait—
The lights are put out early,
The fireflies light up late.

I roused her sleeping bosom
Right early in our walk;
Her heart unfolded for me
Like hyacinths on the stalk.
Her starchy skirts kept rustling
And crackled in my ears
Like sheets of silk cut crosswise
At once by twenty shears.

The dark unsilvered treetops
Grew tall, as on we strode;
Dogs barked, a whole horizon,
Far from the river road.

When we had passed the brambles
And the thickets on our round,
Her coiled hair made a pillow
In a hollow on the ground:
As I undid my necktie,
Her petticoats left their place;

I shed my leather holster,
And she, four layers of lace.

Not nard nor snail had ever
Texture of skin so fine,
Nor crystal in the moonlight
Glimmered with purer shine:
Her thighs slipped from beneath me
Like little trout in fright,
Half chilly (but not frigid),
Half full of shining light.

The whole night saw me posting
Upon my lovely mare;
Mother-of-pearl the saddle,
No need for bridle and spur;
And what her whispers told me
A man should not repeat
When perfect understanding
Has made the mind discreet.

Dirty with sand and kisses
I brought her from the shore
As the iris poised green sabres
At the night wind once more.

To act in decent fashion
As loyal gypsy should,
I gave her a sewing-basket,

Satin and straw, and good;
And yet I would not love her
In spite of what she said
When I took her to the river,
For she was not unwed.

My Last Afternoon with
Uncle Devereux Winslow

1922: the stone porch of my Grandfather's summer house

I

"I won't go with you. I want to stay with Grandpa!"
That's how I threw cold water
on my Mother and Father's
watery martini pipe dreams at Sunday dinner.
. . . Fontainebleau, Mattapoisett, Puget Sound. . . .
Nowhere was anywhere after a summer
at my Grandfather's farm.
Diamond-pointed, athirst and Norman,
its alley of poplars
paraded from Grandmother's rose garden
to a scarey stand of virgin pine,
scrub, and paths forever pioneering.

One afternoon in 1922,
I sat on the stone porch, looking through
screens as black-grained as drifting coal.
Tockytock, tockytock
clumped our Alpine, Edwardian cuckoo clock,
slung with strangled, wooden game.
Our farmer was cementing a root-house under the hill.
One of my hands was cool on a pile
of black earth, the other warm
on a pile of lime. All about me
were the works of my Grandfather's hands:
snapshots of his *Liberty Bell* silver mine;
his high school at *Stukkert am Neckar*;
stogie-brown beams; fools'-gold nuggets;

octagonal red tiles,
sweaty with a secret dank, crummy with ant-stale;
a Rocky Mountain chaise longue,
its legs, shellacked saplings.
A pastel-pale Huckleberry Finn
fished with a broom straw in a basin
hollowed out of a millstone.
Like my Grandfather, the décor
was manly, comfortable,
overbearing, disproportioned.

What were those sunflowers? Pumpkins floating shoulder-high?
It was sunset, Sadie and Nellie
bearing pitchers of ice-tea,
oranges, lemons, mint, and peppermints,
and the jug of shandygaff,
which Grandpa made by blending half and half
yeasty, wheezing homemade sarsaparilla with beer.
The farm, entitled *Char-de-sa*
in the Social Register,
was named for my Grandfather's children:
Charlotte, Devereux, and Sarah.
No one had died there in my lifetime . . .
Only Cinder, our Scottie puppy
paralysed from gobbling toads.
I sat mixing black earth and lime.

II

I was five and a half.
My formal pearl gray shorts
had been worn for three minutes.
My perfection was the Olympian
poise of my models in the imperishable autumn
display windows
of Rogers Peet's boy's store below the State House
in Boston. Distorting drops of water
pinpricked my face in the basin's mirror.
I was a stuffed toucan
with a bibulous, multicolored beak.

III

Up in the air
by the lakeview window in the billiards-room,
lurid in the doldrums of the sunset hour,
my Great Aunt Sarah
was learning *Samson and Delilah*.
She thundered on the keyboard of her dummy piano,
with gauze curtains like a boudoir table,
accordionlike yet soundless.
It had been bought to spare the nerves
of my Grandmother,
tone-deaf, quick as a cricket,
now needing a fourth for "Auction,"

and casting a thirsty eye
on Aunt Sarah, risen like the phoenix
from her bed of troublesome snacks and Tauchnitz classics.

Forty years earlier,
twenty, auburn headed,
grasshopper notes of genius!
Family gossip says Aunt Sarah
tilted her archaic Athenian nose
and jilted an Astor.
Each morning she practiced
on the grand piano at Symphony Hall,
deathlike in the off-season summer—
its naked Greek statues draped with purple
like the saints in Holy Week. . . .
On the recital day, she failed to appear.

IV

I picked with a clean finger nail at the blue anchor
on my sailor blouse washed white as a spinnaker.
What in the world was I wishing?
. . . A sail-colored horse browsing in the bullrushes. . .
A fluff of the west wind puffing
my blouse, kiting me over our seven chimneys,
troubling the waters. . . .
As small as sapphires were the ponds: *Quittacus, Snippituit,*
and *Assawompset,* halved by "the Island,"

where my Uncle's duck blind
floated in a barrage of smoke-clouds.
Double-barrelled shotguns
stuck out like bundles of baby crow-bars.
A single sculler in a camouflaged kayak
was quacking to the decoys. . . .

At the cabin between the waters,
the nearest windows were already boarded.
Uncle Devereux was closing camp for the winter.
As if posed for "the engagement photograph,"
he was wearing his severe
war-uniform of a volunteer Canadian officer.
Daylight from the doorway riddled his student posters,
tacked helter-skelter on walls as raw as a board-walk.
Mr. Punch, a water melon in hockey tights,
was tossing off a decanter of Scotch.
La Belle France in a red, white and blue toga
was accepting the arm of her "protector,"
the ingenu and porcine Edward VII.
The pre-war music hall belles
had goose necks, glorious signatures, beauty-moles,
and coils of hair like rooster tails.
The finest poster was two or three young men in khaki kilts
being bushwhacked on the veldt—
They were almost life-size. . . .

My Uncle was dying at twenty-nine.
"You are behaving like children,"

said my Grandfather,
when my Uncle and Aunt left their three baby daughters,
and sailed for Europe on a last honeymoon . . .
I cowered in terror.
I wasn't a child at all—
unseen and all-seeing, I was Agrippina
in the Golden House of Nero. . . .
Near me was the white measuring-door
my Grandfather had pencilled with my Uncle's heights.
In 1911, he had stopped growing at just six feet.
While I sat on the tiles,
and dug at the anchor on my sailor blouse,
Uncle Devereux stood behind me.
He was as brushed as Bayard, our riding horse.
His face was putty.
His blue coat and white trousers
grew sharper and straighter.
His coat was a blue jay's tail,
his trousers were solid cream from the top of the bottle.
He was animated, hierarchical,
like a ginger snap man in a clothes-press.
He was dying of the incurable Hodgkin's disease. . . .
My hands were warm, then cool, on the piles
of earth and lime,
a black pile and a white pile. . . .
Come winter,
Uncle Devereux would blend to the one color.

JAMES MERRILL

The Broken Home

Crossing the street,
I saw the parents and the child
At their window, gleaming like fruit
With evening's mild gold leaf.

In a room on the floor below,
Sunless, cooler—a brimming
Saucer of wax, marbly and dim—
I have lit what's left of my life.

I have thrown out yesterday's milk
And opened a book of maxims.
The flame quickens. The word stirs.

Tell me, tongue of fire,
That you and I are as real
At least as the people upstairs.

My father, who had flown in World War I,
Might have continued to invest his life
In cloud banks well above Wall Street and wife.
But the race was run below, and the point was to win.

Too late now, I make out in his blue gaze
(Through the smoked glass of being thirty-six)
The soul eclipsed by twin black pupils, sex
And business; time was money in those days.

Each thirteenth year he married. When he died
There were already several chilled wives
In sable orbit—rings, cars, permanent waves.
We'd felt him warming up for a green bride.

He could afford it. He was "in his prime"
At three score ten. But money was not time.

When my parents were younger this was a popular act:
A veiled woman would leap from an electric, wine-dark car
To the steps of no matter what—the Senate or the
    Ritz Bar—
And bodily, at newsreel speed, attack

No matter whom—Al Smith or José Maria Sert
Or Clemenceau—veins standing out on her throat
As she yelled *War mongerer! Pig! Give us the vote!*,
And would have to be hauled away in her hobble skirt.

What had the man done? Oh, made history.
Her business (he had implied) was giving birth,
Tending the house, mending the socks.

Always that same old story—
Father Time and Mother Earth,
A marriage on the rocks.

One afternoon, red, satyr-thighed
Michael, the Irish setter, head
Passionately lowered, led
The child I was to a shut door. Inside,

Blinds beat sun from the bed.
The green-gold room throbbed like a bruise.
Under a sheet, clad in taboos
Lay whom we sought, her hair undone, outspread,

And of a blackness found, if ever now, in old
Engravings where the acid bit.
I must have needed to touch it
Or the whiteness—was she dead?
Her eyes flew open, startled strange and cold.
The dog slumped to the floor. She reached for me. I fled.

Tonight they have stepped out onto the gravel.
The party is over. It's the fall
Of 1931. They love each other still.

She: Charlie, I can't stand the pace.
He: Come on, honey—why, you'll bury us all!

A lead soldier guards my windowsill:
Khaki rifle, uniform, and face.
Something in me grows heavy, silvery, pliable.

How intensely people used to feel!
Like metal poured at the close of a proletarian novel,
Refined and glowing from the crucible,
I see those two hearts, I'm afraid,
Still. Cool here in the graveyard of good and evil,
They are even so to be honored and obeyed.

. . . Obeyed, at least, inversely. Thus
I rarely buy a newspaper, or vote.
To do so, I have learned, is to invite
The tread of a stone guest within my house.

Shooting this rusted bolt, though, against him,
I trust I am no less time's child than some
Who on the heath impersonate Poor Tom
Or on the barricades risk life and limb.

Nor do I try to keep a garden, only
An avocado in a glass of water—
Roots pallid, gemmed with air. And later,

When the small gilt leaves have grown
Fleshy and green, I let them die, yes, yes,
And start another. I am earth's no less.

A child, a red dog roam the corridors,
Still, of the broken home. No sound. The brilliant
Rag runners halt before wide-open doors.
My old room! Its wallpaper—cream, medallioned

With pink and brown—brings back the first nightmares,
Long summer colds, and Emma, sepia-faced,
Perspiring over broth carried upstairs
Aswim with golden fats I could not taste.

The real house became a boarding-school.
Under the ballroom ceiling's allegory
Someone at last may actually be allowed
To learn something; or, from my window, cool
With the unstiflement of the entire story,
Watch a red setter stretch and sink in cloud.

W .   S .   M E R W I N

Vixen

Comet of stillness princess of what is over
    high note held without trembling without voice without sound
aura of complete darkness keeper of the kept secrets
    of the destroyed stories the escaped dreams the sentences
never caught in words warden of where the river went
    touch of its surface sibyl of the extinguished
window onto the hidden place and the other time
    at the foot of the wall by the road patient without waiting
in the full moonlight of autumn at the hour when I was born
    you no longer go out like a flame at the sight of me
you are still warmer than the moonlight gleaming on you
    even now you are unharmed even now perfect
as you have always been now when your light paws are running
    on the breathless night on the bridge with one end I remember
        you
when I have heard you the soles of my feet have made answer
    when I have seen you I have waked and slipped from the
        calendars
from the creeds of difference and the contradictions
    that were my life and all the crumbling fabrications
as long as it lasted until something that we were
    had ended when you are no longer anything
let me catch sight of you again going over the wall
    and before the garden is extinct and the woods are figures
guttering on a screen let my words find their own
    places in the silence after the animals

HENRI MICHAUX

Translated from the French by Richard Ellmann

"I Am Writing to You from a Far-off Country"

I

We have here, she said, only one sun in the month, and for only a little while. We rub our eyes days ahead. But to no purpose. Inexorable weather. Sunlight arrives only at its proper hour.

Then we have a world of things to do, so long as there is light, in fact we hardly have time to look at one another a bit.

The trouble is that nighttime is when we must work, and we really must: dwarfs are born constantly.

II

When you walk in the country, she further confided to him, you may chance to meet with substantial masses on your road. These are mountains and sooner or later you must bend the knee to them. Resisting will do no good, you could go no farther, even by hurting yourself.

I do not say this in order to wound. I could say other things if I really wanted to wound.

III

The dawn is grey here, she went on to tell him. It was not always like this. We do not know whom to accuse.

At night the cattle make a great bellowing, long and flutelike at the end. We feel compassionate, but what can we do?

The smell of eucalyptus surrounds us: a blessing—serenity, but it cannot protect us from everything, or else do you think that it really can protect us from everything?

IV

I add one further word to you, a question rather.

Does water flow in your country too? (I don't remember whether you've told me so) and it gives chills too, if it is the real thing.

Do I love it? I don't know. One feels so alone when it is cold. But quite otherwise when it is warm. Well then? How can I decide? How do you others decide, tell me, when you speak of it without disguise, with open heart?

V

I am writing to you from the end of the world. You must realize this. The trees often tremble. We collect the leaves. They have a ridiculous number of veins. But what for? There's nothing between them and the tree any more, and we go off troubled.

Could not life continue on earth without wind? Or must everything tremble, always, always?

There are subterranean disturbances, too, in the house as well, like angers which might come to face you, like stern beings who would like to wrest confessions.

We see nothing, except what is so unimportant to see.

Nothing, and yet we tremble. Why?

VI

We women here all live with tightened throats. Do you know, although I am very young, in other days I was still younger, and my companions were too. What does that mean? There is surely something horrible in it.

And in other days when, as I have already told you, we were younger still, we were afraid. Someone might have taken advantage of our confusion. Someone might have said to us: "You see, we're going to bury you. The moment has arrived." We were thinking: "It's true, we might just as well be buried this evening, if it is definitely stated that this is the moment."

And we did not dare run too much: Out of breath, at the end of a race, arriving in front of a ditch all prepared, and no time to say a word, no breath.

Tell me, just what is the secret in regard to this?

VII

There are constantly, she told him further, lions in the village, who walk about without any hindrance at all. On condition that we pay no attention to them, they pay no attention to us.

But if they see a young woman running in front of them, they have no desire to apologize for her anxiety. No! They devour her at once.

That is why they constantly walk about the village where they have nothing to do, for quite obviously they might yawn just as well elsewhere.

VIII

For a long, long time, she confided to him, we have been in combat with the sea.

On the very rare occasions when she is blue, soft, one might suppose her to be happy. But that would not last. Her smell says so anyway, a smell of rot (if it is not her bitterness).

Here I should explain the matter of the waves. It is terribly complicated, and the sea . . . I implore you, have confidence in me. Would I want to deceive you? She is not only a word. She is not only a fear. She exists; I swear it to you; one sees her constantly.

Who? Why, we, we see her. She comes from far away to wrangle with us and to terrify us.

When you come you will see for yourself, you will be very startled. "Well, I'll be . . .!" you'll say, for she is stupefying.

We'll look at her together. I am sure I will not be afraid. Tell me, will this never happen?

IX

I cannot leave you with a doubt, she continues, with a lack of confidence. I should like to speak to you again of the sea. But the obstacle remains. The streams go forward; but not she. Listen, don't be angry, I swear it to you, I wouldn't dream of deceiving you. She is like that. No matter how excited she gets, she will halt before a little sand. She's a great falterer. She would certainly like to go forward, but there's the story.

Later on, maybe, some day she will go forward.

X

"We are more than ever surrounded by ants," says her letter. They push the dust uneasily at top speed. They take no interest in us.

Not one raises its head.

This is the most tightly closed society that could exist, although outdoors they spread out constantly in all directions. No matter, their projected schemes, their preoccupations . . . they are among themselves . . . everywhere.

And up to the present time not one has raised its head towards us. It would rather be crushed.

XI

She writes to him again:

"You cannot imagine all that there is in the sky, you would have to see it to believe it. So now, the . . . but I'm not going to tell you their name at once."

In spite of their air of weighing a great deal and of occupying almost all the sky, they do not weigh, huge though they are, as much as a newborn baby.

We call them clouds.

It is true that water comes out of them, but not by compressing them, or by pounding them. It would be useless, they have so little.

But, by reason of their occupying lengths and lengths, widths and widths, deeps also and deeps, and of puffing themselves up, they succeed in the long run in making a few droplets of water fall, yes, of water. And we are really wet. We run off furious at having been trapped; for nobody knows the moment when they are going to release their drops; sometimes they rest for days without releasing them. And one would stay home waiting for them in vain.

XII

The education regarding chills is not well handled in this country. We are ignorant of the true rules and when the event appears, we are taken unawares.

It is Time, of course. (Is it the same with you?) One must arrive a little sooner than it does; you see what I mean, only a tiny little bit ahead. You know the story of the flea in the drawer? Yes, of course. And how true it is, don't you think! I don't know what more to say. When are we going to see each other at last?

The Cameo

Forever over now, forever, forever gone
That day. Clear and diminished like a scene
Carven in cameo, the lighthouse, and the cove between
The sandy cliffs, and the boat drawn up on the beach;
And the long skirt of a lady innocent and young,
Her hand resting on her bosom, her head hung;
And the figure of a man in earnest speech.

Clear and diminished like a scene cut in cameo
The lighthouse, and the boat on the beach, and the two shapes
Of the woman and the man; lost like the lost day
Are the words that passed, and the pain,—discarded, cut away
From the stone, as from the memory the heat of the tears escapes.

O troubled forms, O early love unfortunate and hard,
Time has estranged you into a jewel cold and pure;
From the action of the waves and from the action of sorrow forever
    secure,
White against a ruddy cliff you stand, chalcedony on sard.

CZESŁAW MIŁOSZ

Translated from the Polish by Czesław Miłosz and Lillian Vallee

Encounter

We were riding through frozen fields in a wagon at dawn.
A red wing rose in the darkness.

And suddenly a hare ran across the road.
One of us pointed to it with his hand.

That was long ago. Today neither of them is alive,
Not the hare, nor the man who made the gesture.

O my love, where are they, where are they going
The flash of a hand, streak of movement, rustle of pebbles.
I ask not out of sorrow, but in wonder.

Wilno, 1936

CZESŁAW MIŁOSZ

Translated from the Polish by Czesław Miłosz and Lawrence Davis

Elegy for N. N.

Tell me if it is too far for you.
You could have run over the small waves of the Baltic
and past the fields of Denmark, past a beech wood
could have turned toward the ocean, and there, very soon
Labrador, white at this season.
And if you, who dreamed about a lonely island,
were frightened of cities and of lights flashing along the highway
you had a path straight through the wilderness
over blue-black, melting waters, with tracks of deer and caribou
as far as the Sierras and abandoned gold mines.
The Sacramento River could have led you
between hills overgrown with prickly oaks.
Then just a eucalyptus grove, and you had found me.

True, when the manzanita is in bloom
and the bay is clear on spring mornings
I think reluctantly of the house between the lakes
and of nets drawn in beneath the Lithuanian sky.
The bath cabin where you used to leave your dress
has changed forever into an abstract crystal.
Honey-like darkness is there, near the veranda,
and comic young owls, and the scent of leather.

How could one live at that time, I really can't say.
Styles and dresses flicker, indistinct,
not self-sufficient, tending toward a finale.
Does it matter that we long for things as they are in themselves?

The knowledge of fiery years has scorched the horses standing at
    the forge,
the little columns in the marketplace,
the wooden stairs and the wig of Mama Fliegeltaub.

We learned so much, this you know well:
how, gradually, what could not be taken away
is taken. People, countrysides.
And the heart does not die when one thinks it should,
we smile, there is tea and bread on the table.
And only remorse that we did not love
the poor ashes in Sachsenhausen
with absolute love, beyond human power.

You got used to new, wet winters,
to a villa where the blood of the German owner
was washed from the wall, and he never returned.
I too accepted but what was possible, cities and countries.
One cannot step twice into the same lake
on rotting alder leaves,
breaking a narrow sunstreak.

Guilt, yours and mine? Not a great guilt.
Secrets, yours and mine? Not great secrets.
Not when they bind the jaw with a kerchief, put a little cross
    between the fingers,
and somewhere a dog barks, and the first star flares up.

No, it was not because it was too far
you failed to visit me that day or night.
From year to year it grows in us until it takes hold,
I understood it as you did: indifference.

Berkeley, 1963

EUGENIO MONTALE

Translated from the Italian by Charles Wright

The Eel

The eel, siren
of the cold seas, who leaves her Baltic playground
for our warm waters, our estuaries,
our rivers, who cuts through their deepest soundings,
against their angry tides, from branch to branch,
from stem to stem as they thin,
farther and farther inward, snaking
into the heart of the rocky landscape, worming
through the arteries of slime until one day
a blaze, struck from the chestnut blossoms,
flares her tracks through the pools of dead water.
in the ruts cut out of the cliffs
which fall away from the Apennines to the Romagna;
the eel, whiplash, twisting torch,
love's arrow on earth, which only
our gullies and dried-out, burned-out streams
can lead to the paradises of fecundity;
green spirit that hunts for life
only there, where drought and desolation gnaw,
a spark that says everything starts
where everything is charred, stumps buried;
vanishing rainbow, twin sister
to her you set behind your own eyelids
and let shine out over the sons of men, on us
up to our hairlines in your breathing mud . . .
and *you* can't call her sister?

The Fish

wade
through black jade.
   Of the crow-blue mussel-shells, one keeps
   adjusting the ash-heaps;
      opening and shutting itself like

an
injured fan.
   The barnacles which encrust the side
   of the wave, cannot hide
      there for the submerged shafts of the

sun,
split like spun
   glass, move themselves with spotlight swiftness
   into the crevices—
      in and out, illuminating

the
turquoise sea
   of bodies. The water drives a wedge
   of iron through the iron edge
      of the cliff; whereupon the stars,

pink
rice-grains, ink-
   bespattered jelly-fish, crabs like green
   lilies, and submarine
      toadstools, slide each on the other.

All
external
    marks of abuse are present on this
    defiant edifice—
        all the physical features of

ac-
cident—lack
    of cornice, dynamite grooves, burns, and
    hatchet strokes, these things stand
        out on it; the chasm-side is

dead.
Repeated
    evidence has proved that it can live
    on what can not revive
        its youth. The sea grows old in it.

The Absent

They are not here. And we, we are the Others
Who walk by ourselves unquestioned in the sun
Which shines for us and only for us.
For They are not here.
And are made known to us in this great absence
That lies upon us and is between us
Since They are not here.
Now, in this kingdom of summer idleness
Where slowly we the sun-tranced multitudes dream and wander
In deep oblivion of brightness
And breathe ourselves out, out into the air—
It is absence that receives us;
We do not touch, our souls go out in the absence
That lies between us and is about us.
For we are the Others,
And so we sorrow for These that are not with us,
Not knowing we sorrow or that this is our sorrow,
Since it is long past thought or memory or device of mourning,
Sorrow for loss of that which we never possessed,
The unknown, the nameless,
The ever-present that in their absence are with us
(With us the inheritors, the usurpers, claiming
The sun and the kingdom of the sun) that sorrow
And loneliness might bring a blessing upon us.

OGDEN NASH

Very Like a Whale

One thing that literature would be greatly the better for
Would be a more restricted employment by authors of simile and
    metaphor.
Authors of all races, be they Greeks, Romans, Teutons or Celts,
Can't seem just to say that anything is the thing it is but have to go
    out of their way to say that it is like something else.
What does it mean when we are told
That the Assyrian came down like a wolf on the fold?
In the first place, George Gordon Byron had had enough
    experience
To know that it probably wasn't just one Assyrian, it was a lot of
    Assyrians.
However, as too many arguments are apt to induce apoplexy and
    thus hinder longevity,
We'll let it pass as one Assyrian for the sake of brevity.
Now then, this particular Assyrian, the one whose cohorts were
    gleaming in purple and gold,
Just what does the poet mean when he says he came down like a
    wolf on the fold?
In heaven and earth more than is dreamed of in our philosophy
    there are a great many things,
But I don't imagine that among them there is a wolf with purple
    and gold cohorts or purple and gold anythings.
No, no, Lord Byron, before I'll believe that this Assyrian was
    actually like a wolf I must have some kind of proof;
Did he run on all fours and did he have a hairy tail and a big red
    mouth and big white teeth and did he say Woof woof woof?
Frankly I think it very unlikely, and all you were entitled to say, at
    the very most,

Was that the Assyrian cohorts came down like a lot of Assyrian
    cohorts about to destroy the Hebrew host.
But that wasn't fancy enough for Lord Byron, oh dear me no,
    he had to invent a lot of figures of speech and then interpolate
    them,
With the result that whenever you mention Old Testament soldiers
    to people they say Oh yes, they're the ones that a lot of wolves
    dressed up in gold and purple ate them.
That's the kind of thing that's being done all the time by poets,
    from Homer to Tennyson;
They're always comparing ladies to lilies and veal to venison.
How about the man who wrote,
Her little feet stole in and out like mice beneath her petticoat?
Wouldn't anybody but a poet think twice
Before stating that his girl's feet were mice?
Then they always say things like that after a winter storm
The snow is a white blanket. Oh it is, is it, all right then, you sleep
    under a six-inch blanket of snow and I'll sleep under a half-inch
    blanket of unpoetical blanket material and we'll see which one
    keeps warm,
And after that maybe you'll begin to comprehend dimly
What I mean by too much metaphor and simile.

PABLO NERUDA

Translated from the Spanish by Margaret Sayers Peden

Ode to the Seagull

To the seagull
high above
the pinewoods
of the coast,
on the wind
the sibilant
syllable of my ode.

Sail,
bright boat,
winged banner,
in my verse,
stitch,
body of silver,
your emblem
across the shirt
of the icy firmament,
oh, aviator,
gentle
serenade of flight,
snow arrow, serene
ship in the transparent storm,
steady, you soar
while
the hoarse wind sweeps
the meadows of the sky.

After your long voyage,
feathered magnolia,

triangle borne
aloft on the air,
slowly you regain
your form,
arranging
your silvery robes, shaping
your bright treasure in an oval,
again a
white bud of flight,
a round
seed,
egg of beauty.

Another
poet
would end here
his triumphant ode.
I cannot
limit myself
to
the luxurious whiteness
of useless froth.
Forgive me,
seagull,
I am
a realist
poet,
photographer of the sky.
You eat,

and eat,
and eat,
there is nothing
you don't devour,
on the waters of the bay
you bark
like a beggar's dog,
you pursue
the last
scrap of
fish gut,
you peck
at your white sisters,
you steal
your despicable prize,
a rotting clump
of floating garbage,
decayed
tomatoes,
the discarded
rubbish of the cove.
But
in you
it is transformed
into clean wing,
white geometry,
the ecstatic line of flight.

That is why,
snowy anchor,
aviator,
I celebrate you as you are:
your insatiable voraciousness,
your screech in the rain,
or at rest
a snowflake blown
from the storm,
at peace or in flight,
seagull,
I consecrate to you
my earthbound words,
my clumsy attempt at flight;
let's see whether you scatter
your birdseed in my ode.

To the Film Industry in Crisis

Not you, lean quarterlies and swarthy periodicals
with your studious incursions toward the pomposity of ants,
nor you, experimental theatre in which Emotive Fruition
is wedding Poetic Insight perpetually, nor you,
promenading Grand Opera, obvious as an ear (though you
are close to my heart), but you, Motion Picture Industry,
it's you I love!

In times of crisis, we must all decide again and again whom we love.
And give credit where it's due: not to my starched nurse, who
    taught me
how to be bad and not bad rather than good (and has lately availed
herself of this information), not to the Catholic Church
which is at best an oversolemn introduction to cosmic
    entertainment,
not to the American Legion, which hates everybody, but to you,
glorious Silver Screen, tragic Technicolor, amorous Cinemascope,
stretching Vistavision and startling Stereophonic Sound, with all
your heavenly dimensions and reverberations and iconoclasms! To
Richard Barthelmess as the "tol'able" boy barefoot and in pants,
Jeanette MacDonald of the flaming hair and lips and long, long neck,
Sue Carroll as she sits for eternity on the damaged fender of a car
and smiles, Ginger Rogers with her pageboy bob like a sausage
on her shuffling shoulders, peach-melba-voiced Fred Astaire of the
    feet,
Eric von Stroheim, the seducer of mountain-climbers' gasping
    spouses,
The Tarzans, each and every one of you (I cannot bring myself to
    prefer

Johnny Weissmuller to Lex Barker, I cannot!), Mae West in a furry
    sled,
her bordello radiance and bland remarks, Rudolph Valentino of the
    moon,
its crushing passions, and moonlike, too, the gentle Norma Shearer,
Miriam Hopkins dropping her champagne glass off Joel McCrea's
    yacht
and crying into the dappled sea, Clark Gable rescuing Gene Tierney
from Russia and Allan Jones rescuing Kitty Carlisle from Harpo
    Marx,
Cornel Wilde coughing blood on the piano keys while Merle
    Oberon berates,
Marilyn Monroe in her little spike heels reeling through Niagara
    Falls,
Joseph Cotton puzzling and Orson Welles puzzled and Dolores
    del Rio
eating orchids for lunch and breaking mirrors, Gloria Swanson
    reclining,
and Jean Harlow reclining and wiggling, and Alice Faye reclining
and wiggling and singing, Myrna Loy being calm and wise, William
    Powell
in his stunning urbanity, Elizabeth Taylor blossoming, yes, to you

and to all you others, the great, the near-great, the featured, the
    extras
who pass quickly and return in dreams saying your one or two lines,
my love!
Long may you illumine space with your marvellous appearances,
    delays

and enunciations, and may the money of the world glitteringly
   cover you
as you rest after a long day under the kleig lights with your faces
in packs for our edification, the way the clouds come often at
   night
but the heavens operate on the star system. It is a divine precedent
you perpetuate! Roll on, reels of celluloid, as the great earth rolls
   on!

The Undertaking in New Jersey

Beyond the Hudson's
Unimportant water lapping
In the dark against the city's shores
Are the small towns, remnants
Of forge and coal yard. The bird's voice in their streets
May not mean much: a bird the age of a child chirping
At curbs and curb gratings,
As barber shops and townsmen
Born of girls—
Of girls! Girls gave birth . . . But the interiors
Are the women's: curtained,
Lit, the fabric
To which the men return. Surely they imagine
Some task beyond the window glass
And the fabrics as if an eventual brother
In the fields were nourished by all this in country
Torn by the trucks where towns
And the flat boards of homes
Visibly move at sunrise and the trees
Carry quickly into daylight the excited birds.

Anthem for Doomed Youth

What passing-bells for these who die as cattle?
   Only the monstrous anger of the guns.
   Only the stuttering rifles' rapid rattle
Can patter out their hasty orisons.
No mockeries for them from prayers or bells,
   Nor any voice of mourning save the choirs,—
The shrill, demented choirs of wailing shells;
   And bugles calling for them from sad shires.

What candles may be held to speed them all?
   Not in the hands of boys, but in their eyes
Shall shine the holy glimmers of good-byes.
   The pallor of girls' brows shall be their pall
Their flowers the tenderness of silent minds,
And each slow dusk a drawing-down of blinds.

DAN PAGIS
Translated from the Hebrew by Stephen Mitchell

Ein Leben

In the month of her death, she is standing by the windowframe,
a young woman with a stylish, permanent wave.
She seems to be in a contemplative mood
as she stands there looking out the window.

Through the glass an afternoon cloud of 1934
looks in at her, blurred, slightly out of focus,
but her faithful servant. On the inside
I'm the one looking at her, four years old almost,

holding back my ball, quietly
going out of the photo and growing old,
growing old carefully, quietly,
so as not to frighten her.

NICANOR PARRA
Translated from the Spanish by W. S. Merwin

The Tunnel

In my youth I lived for a time in the house of some aunts
On the heels of the death of a gentleman with whom they had been
      intimately connected
Whose ghost tormented them without pity
Making life intolerable for them.

At the beginning I ignored their telegrams
And their letters composed in the language of another day,
Larded with mythological allusions
And proper names that meant nothing to me
Some referring to sages of antiquity
Or minor medieval philosophers
Or merely to neighbors.

To give up the university just like that
And break off the joys of a life of pleasure,
To put a stop to it all
In order to placate the caprices of three hysterical old women
Riddled with every kind of personal difficulty,
This, to a person of my character, seemed
An uninspiring prospect,
A brainless idea.

Four years, just the same, I lived in The Tunnel
In the company of those frightening old ladies,
Four years of uninterrupted torture
Morning, noon, and night.
The delightful hours that I had spent under the trees
Were duly replaced by weeks of revulsion,

Months of anguish, which I did my best to disguise
For fear of attracting their curiosity.
They stretched into years of ruin and misery.
For centuries my soul was imprisoned
In a bottle of drinking water!

My spiritualist conception of the world
Left me obviously inferior to every fact I was faced with:
I saw everything through a prism
In the depths of which the images of my aunts intertwined
        like living threads
Forming a sort of impenetrable chain mail
Which hurt my eyes, making them more and more useless.

A young man of scanty means can't work things out
He lives in a bell jar called Art
Or Pleasure or Science
Trying to make contact with a world of relationships
That only exist for him and a small group of friends.

Under the influence of a sort of water vapor
That found its way through the floor of the room
Flooding the atmosphere till it blotted out everything
I spent the nights at my work table
Absorbed in practicing automatic writing.

But why rake deeper into this wretched affair?
Those old women led me on disgracefully
With their false promises, with their weird fantasies,

With their cleverly performed sufferings.
They managed to keep me enmeshed for years
Making me feel obliged to work for them, though it was never said:
Agricultural labors,
Purchase and sale of cattle,
Until one night, looking through the keyhole
I noticed that one of my aunts—
The paralytic—
Was getting about beautifully on the tips of her toes,
And I came to, knowing I'd been bewitched.

BORIS PASTERNAK

Translated from the Russian by Richard McKane

Winter Night

Snow, snow over the whole land
across all boundaries.
The candle burned on the table,
the candle burned.

As in summer swarms
of midges fly to a flame,
snowflakes fluttered
around the windowframe.

Blown snow stuck
rings and arrows on the glass.
The candle burned on the table,
the candle burned.

Shadows were lying
on the lighted ceiling,
of crossed arms, crossed legs,
crossed destinies.

Two shoes fell
noisily on the floor.
The night light wept
wax drops on a dress.

Everything was lost in the
greying white snow haze.
The candle burned on the table,
the candle burned.

Draught at the candle from the corner,
the heat of temptation
angel-like raised two wings
in the form of a cross.

Snow fell all February
and now and then
the candle burned on the table,
the candle burned.

CESARE PAVESE

Translated from the Italian by William Arrowsmith

Morning Star

The man alone gets up while the sea's still dark
and the stars still flicker. A warmth like breathing
drifts from the shore where the sea has its bed,
sweetening the air he breathes. This is the hour when nothing
can happen. Even the pipe dangling from his teeth
is out. The sea at night makes a muffled plash.
By now the man alone has kindled a big fire of brush,
he watches it redden the ground. Before long
the sea will be like the fire, a blaze of heat.

Nothing's more bitter than the dawning of a day
when nothing will happen. Nothing's more bitter
than being useless. A greenish star, surprised
by the dawn, still droops feebly in the sky.
It looks down on the sea, still dark, and the brushwood fire
where the man, simply to do something, is warming himself.
It looks, then drops sleepily down among the dusky mountains
to its bed of snow. The hour drags by, cruelly
slow for a man who's waiting for nothing at all.

Why should the sun bother to rise from the sea
or the long day bother to begin? Tomorrow
the warm dawn with its transparent light will be back,
and everything will be like yesterday, and nothing will happen.
The man alone would like nothing more than to sleep.
When the last star in the sky is quenched and gone,
the man quietly tamps his tobacco and lights his pipe.

OCTAVIO PAZ

Translated from the Spanish by Elliot Weinberger

As One Listens to the Rain

Listen to me as one listens to the rain,
not attentive, not distracted,
light footsteps, thin drizzle,
water that is air, air that is time,
the day is still leaving,
the night has yet to arrive,
figurations of mist
at the turn of the corner,
figurations of time
at the bend in this pause,
listen to me as one listens to the rain,
without listening, hear what I say
with eyes open inward, asleep
with all five senses awake,
it's raining, light footsteps, a murmur of syllables,
air and water, words with no weight:
what we were and are,
the days and years, this moment,
weightless time and heavy sorrow,
listen to me as one listens to the rain,
wet asphalt is shining,
steam rises and walks away,
night unfolds and looks at me,
you are you and your body of steam,
you and your face of night,
you and your hair, unhurried lightning,
you cross the street and enter my forehead,
footsteps of water across my eyes,
listen to me as one listens to the rain,

the asphalt's shining, you cross the street,
it is the mist, wandering in the night,
it is the night, asleep in your bed,
it is the surge of waves in your breath,
your fingers of water dampen my forehead,
your fingers of flame burn my eyes,
your fingers of air open eyelids of time,
a spring of visions and resurrections,
listen to me as one listens to the rain,
the years go by, the moments return,
do you hear your footsteps in the next room?
not here, not there: you hear them
in another time that is now,
listen to the footsteps of time,
inventor of places with no weight, nowhere,
listen to the rain running over the terrace,
the night is now more night in the grove,
lightning has nestled among the leaves,
a restless garden adrift—go in,
your shadow covers this page.

FERNANDO PESSOA (ÁLVARO DE CAMPOS)
Translated from the Portuguese by Richard Zenith

The Tobacco Shop

I'm nothing.
I'll always be nothing.
I can't want to be something.
But I have in me all the dreams of the world.

Windows of my room,
The room of one of the world's millions nobody knows
(And if they knew me, what would they know?),
You open onto the mystery of a street continually crossed by people,
A street inaccessible to any and every thought,
Real, impossibly real, certain, unknowingly certain,
With the mystery of things beneath the stones and beings,
With death making the walls damp and the hair of men white,
With Destiny driving the wagon of everything down the road of
    nothing.

Today I'm defeated, as if I'd learned the truth.
Today I'm lucid, as if I were about to die
And had no greater kinship with things
Than to say farewell, this building and this side of the street
    becoming
A row of train cars, with the whistle for departure
Blowing in my head
And my nerves jolting and bones creaking as we pull out.

Today I'm bewildered, like a man who wondered and discovered
    and forgot.
Today I'm torn between the loyalty I owe

To the outward reality of the Tobacco Shop across the street
And to the inward reality of my feeling that everything's a dream.

I failed in everything.
Since I had no ambition, perhaps I failed in nothing.
I left the education I was given,
Climbing down from the window at the back of the house.
I went to the country with big plans.
But all I found was grass and trees,
And when there were people they were just like others.
I step back from the window and sit in a chair. What should I
    think about?

How should I know what I'll be, I who don't know what I am?
Be what I think? But I think of being so many things!
And there are so many who think of being the same thing that we
    can't all be it!
Genius? At this moment
A hundred thousand brains are dreaming they're geniuses like me,
And it may be that history won't remember even one,
All of their imagined conquests amounting to so much dung.
No, I don't believe in me.
Insane asylums are full of lunatics with certainties!
Am I, who have no certainties, more right or less right?
No, not even in me . . .
In how many garrets and non-garrets of the world
Are self-convinced geniuses at this moment dreaming?
How many lofty and noble and lucid aspirations

—Yes, truly lofty and noble and lucid
And perhaps even attainable—
Will never see the true light of day or find a sympathetic ear?
The world is for those born to conquer it,
Not for those who dream they can conquer it, even if they're right.
I've done more in dreams than Napoleon.

I've held more humanities against my hypothetical breast than
   Christ.
I've secretly invented philosophies such as Kant never wrote.
But I am, and perhaps will always be, the man in the garret,
Even though I don't live in one.
I'll always be *the one who wasn't born for that*;
I'll always be merely *the one who had qualities*;
I'll always be the one who waited for a door to open in a wall with-
   out doors
And sang the song of the Infinite in a chicken coop
And heard the voice of God in a covered well.
Believe in me? No, not in anything.
Let Nature pour over my seething head
Its sun, its rain, and the wind that finds my hair,
And let the rest come if it will or must, or let it not come.
Cardiac slaves of the stars,
We conquered the whole world before getting out of bed,
But we woke up and it's hazy,
We got up and it's alien,
We went outside and it's the entire earth
Plus the solar system and the Milky Way and the Indefinite.

(Eat your chocolates, little girl,
Eat your chocolates!
Believe me, there's no metaphysics on earth like chocolates,
And all religions put together teach no more than the candy shop.
Eat, dirty little girl, eat!
If only I could eat chocolates with the same truth as you!
But I think and, removing the silver paper that's tinfoil,
I throw it all on the ground, as I've thrown out life.)

But at least, from my bitterness over what I'll never be,
There remains the hasty writing of these verses,
A broken gateway to the Impossible.
But at least I confer on myself a contempt without tears,
Noble at least in the sweeping gesture by which I fling
The dirty laundry that's me—with no list—into the stream of
    things,
And I stay at home, shirtless.

(O my consoler, who doesn't exist and therefore consoles,
Be you a Greek goddess, conceived as a living statue,
Or a patrician woman of Rome, impossibly noble and dire,
Or a princess of the troubadours, all charm and grace,
Or an eighteenth-century marchioness, décolleté and aloof,
Or a famous courtesan from our parents' generation,
Or something modern, I can't quite imagine what—
Whatever all of this is, whatever you are, if you can inspire, then
    inspire me!
My heart is a poured-out bucket.

In the same way invokers of spirits invoke spirits, I invoke
My own self and find nothing.
I go to the window and see the street with absolute clarity.
I see the shops, I see the sidewalks, I see the passing cars,
I see the clothed living beings who pass each other.
I see the dogs that also exist,
And all of this weighs on me like a sentence of exile,
And all of this is foreign, like everything else.)

I've lived, studied, loved, and even believed,
And today there's not a beggar I don't envy just because he isn't me.
I look at the tatters and sores and falsehood of each one,
And I think: perhaps you never lived or studied or loved or believed
(For it's possible to do all of this without having done any of it);
Perhaps you've merely existed, as when a lizard has its tail cut off
And the tail keeps on twitching, without the lizard.
I made of myself what I was no good at making,
And what I could have made of myself I didn't.
I put on the wrong costume
And was immediately taken for someone I wasn't, and I said noth-
    ing and was lost.
When I went to take off the mask,
It was stuck to my face.
When I got it off and saw myself in the mirror,
I had already grown old.
I was drunk and no longer knew how to wear the costume that I
    hadn't taken off.
I threw out the mask and slept in the closet

Like a dog tolerated by the management
Because it's harmless,
And I'll write down this story to prove I'm sublime.

Musical essence of my useless verses,
If only I could look at you as something I had made
Instead of always looking at the Tobacco Shop across the street,
Trampling on my consciousness of existing,
Like a rug a drunkard stumbles on
Or a doormat stolen by gypsies and it's not worth a thing.

But the Tobacco Shop Owner has come to the door and is standing
    there.
I look at him with the discomfort of a half-twisted neck
Compounded by the discomfort of a half-grasping soul.
He will die and I will die.
He'll leave his signboard, I'll leave my poems.
His sign will also eventually die, and so will my poems.
Eventually the street where the sign was will die,
And so will the language in which my poems were written.
Then the whirling planet where all of this happened will die.

On other planets of other solar systems something like people
Will continue to make things like poems and to live under things
    like signs,
Always one thing facing the other,
Always one thing as useless as the other,
Always the impossible as stupid as reality,

Always the inner mystery as true as the mystery sleeping on the
  surface.
Always this thing or always that, or neither one thing nor the
  other.

But a man has entered the Tobacco Shop (to buy tobacco?),
And plausible reality suddenly hits me.
I half rise from my chair—energetic, convinced, human—
And will try to write these verses in which I say the opposite.

I light up a cigarette as I think about writing them,
And in that cigarette I savor a freedom from all thought.
My eyes follow the smoke as if it were my own trail
And I enjoy, for a sensitive and fitting moment,
A liberation from all speculation
And an awareness that metaphysics is a consequence of not feeling
  very well.
Then I lean back in the chair
And keep smoking.
As long as Destiny permits, I'll keep smoking.

(If I married my washwoman's daughter
Perhaps I would be happy.)
I get up from the chair. I go to the window.

The man has come out of the Tobacco Shop (putting change into
  his pocket?).
Ah, I know him: it's unmetaphysical Esteves.
(The Tobacco Shop Owner has come to the door.)

As if by divine instinct, Esteves turns around and sees me.
He waves hello, I shout back "Hello, Esteves!" and the universe
Falls back into place without ideals or hopes, and the Owner of the
    Tobacco Shop smiles.

15 January 1928

FRANCIS PONGE

Translated from the French by Beth Archer Brombert

Water

Below me, always below me is water. Always with lowered eyes do I look at it. It is like the ground, like a part of the ground, a modification of the ground.

It is bright and brilliant, formless and fresh, passive yet persistent in its one vice, gravity; disposing of extraordinary means to satisfy that vice—twisting, piercing, eroding, filtering.

This vice works from within as well: water collapses all the time, constantly sacrifices all form, tends only to humble itself, flattens itself on the ground, like a corpse, like the monks of certain orders. Always lower—that could be its motto; the opposite of excelsior.

*

One might almost say that water is mad, because of its hysterical need to obey gravity alone, a need that possesses it like an obsession.

Of course, everything in the world responds to this need, which always and everywhere must be satisfied. This cabinet, for example, proves to be terribly stubborn in its desire to stay on the ground, and if one day it found itself badly balanced, would sooner fall to pieces than run counter to that desire. But to a certain degree it teases gravity, defies it; does not give way in all its parts: its cornice, its moldings do not give in. Inherent in the cabinet is a resistance that benefits its personality and form.

LIQUID, by definition, is that which chooses to obey gravity rather than maintain its form, which rejects all form in order to obey gravity—and which loses all dignity because of that obsession, that pathological anxiety. Because of that vice—which makes it fast, flowing, or stagnant, formless or fearsome, formless *and* fearsome, piercingly fearsome in cases; devious, filtering, winding—one can do anything one wants with it, even lead water through pipes to make it spout out vertically so as to enjoy the way it collapses in droplets: a real slave.

The sun and the moon, however, are envious of this exclusive influence, and try to take over whenever water happens to offer the opening of great expanses, and above all when in a state of least resistance—spread out in shallow puddles. Then the sun exacts an even greater tribute: forces it into a perpetual cycle, treats it like a gerbil on a wheel.

*

Water eludes me . . . slips between my fingers. And even so! It's not even that clean (like a lizard or a frog): it leaves traces, spots, on my hands that are quite slow to dry or have to be wiped. Water escapes me yet marks me, and there is not a thing I can do about it.

Ideologically it's the same thing: it eludes me, eludes all definition, but in my mind and on this sheet leaves traces, formless marks.

*

Water's instability: sensitive to the slightest change of level. Running down stairs two at a time. Playful, childishly obedient, returning as soon as called if one alters the slope on this side.

VASKO POPA

Translated from the Serbian by Charles Simic

The Little Box

The little box gets her first teeth
And her little length
Little width little emptiness
And all the rest she has

The little box continues growing
The cupboard that she was inside
Is now inside her

And she grows bigger bigger bigger
Now the room is inside her
And the house and the city and the earth
And the world she was in before

The little box remembers her childhood
And by a great great longing
She becomes a little box again

Now in the little box
You have the whole world in miniature
You can easily put it in a pocket
Easily steal it easily lose it

Take care of the little box

EZRA POUND

Canto XLV

With *Usura*

With usura hath no man a house of good stone
each block cut smooth and well fitting
that design might cover their face,
with usura
hath no man a painted paradise on his church wall
harpes et luz
or where virgin receiveth message
and halo projects from incision,
with usura
seeth no man Gonzaga his heirs and his concubines
no picture is made to endure nor to live with
but it is made to sell and sell quickly
with usura, sin against nature,
is thy bread ever more of stale rags
is thy bread dry as paper,
with no mountain wheat, no strong flour
with usura the line grows thick
with usura is no clear demarcation
and no man can find site for his dwelling.
Stonecutter is kept from his stone
weaver is kept from his loom
WITH USURA
wool comes not to market
sheep bringeth no gain with usura
Usura is a murrain, usura
blunteth the needle in the maid's hand
and stoppeth the spinner's cunning. Pietro Lombardo

came not by usura
Duccio came not by usura
nor Pier della Francesca; Zuan Bellin' not by usura
nor was "La Calunnia" painted.
Came not by usura Angelico; came not Ambrogio Praedis,
Came no church of cut stone signed: *Adamo me fecit.*
Not by usura St Trophime
Not by usura Saint Hilaire,
Usura rusteth the chisel
It rusteth the craft and the craftsman
It gnaweth the thread in the loom
None learneth to weave gold in her pattern;
Azure hath a canker by usura; cramoisi is unbroidered
Emerald findeth no Memling
Usura slayeth the child in the womb
It stayeth the young man's courting
It hath brought palsey to bed, lyeth
between the young bride and her bridegroom
                    CONTRA NATURAM
They have brought whores for Eleusis
Corpses are set to banquet
at behest of usura.

N.B. *Usury: A charge for the use of purchasing power, levied without regard to pro-*
duction; often without regard to the possibilities of production. (Hence the failure of
the Medici bank.)

JACQUES PRÉVERT
Translated from the French by Harriet Zinnes

Barbara

Remember Barbara
It rained without letup in Brest that day
And you walked smiling
Glowing ravishing drenched
Under the rain
Remember Barbara
It rained without letup in Brest
And I passed you on the Rue de Siam
You smiled
And I smiled too
Remember Barbara
You whom I did not know
You who did not know me
Remember
Remember that day just the same
Do not forget
A man was taking shelter in a doorway
And he called out your name
Barbara
And you ran toward him under the rain
Drenched ravishing glowing
And you threw yourself into his arms
Remember that Barbara
And do not be angry with me if I call you by your first name
I call all those I love by their first names
Even if I have met them only once
I call all who love by their first names
Even if I do not know them
Remember Barbara

Do not forget
That gentle, happy rain
On your happy face
On that happy town
That rain on the sea
On the arsenal
On the boat of Ouessant
Oh Barbara
What shit war is
What has become of you now
Under the rain of iron
Of fire of steel of blood
And he who held you in his arms
Lovingly
Is he dead missing or still living
Oh Barbara
It rains without letup in Brest
As it rained before
But it is not the same everything is ruined
It is a rain of mourning terrible and desolate
No longer even a storm
Of iron of steel of blood
Only of clouds
That burst
And disappear like dogs
Down the streams of Brest
Like dogs that will rot far away
Far away very far from Brest
Of which there is nothing left

RAYMOND QUENEAU

Translated from the French by Michael Benedikt

If You Imagine

If you imagine
if you imagine
little sweetie little sweetie
if you imagine
this will this will this
will last forever
this season of
this season of
season of love
you're fooling yourself
little sweetie little sweetie
you're fooling yourself

If you think little one
if you think ah ah
that that rosy complexion
that waspy waist
those lovely muscles
the enamel nails
nymph thigh
and your light foot
if you think little one
that will that will that
will last forever
you're fooling yourself
little sweetie little sweetie
you're fooling yourself

The lovely days disappear
the lovely holidays
suns and planets
go round in a circle
but you my little one
you go straight
toward you know not what
very slowly draw near
the sudden wrinkle
the weighty fat
the triple chin
the flabby muscle
come gather gather
the roses the roses
roses of life
and may their petals
be a calm sea
of happinesses
come gather gather
if you don't do it
you're fooling yourself
little sweetie little sweetie
you're fooling yourself

RAINER MARIA RILKE

Translated from the German by Edward Snow

Tombs of the Hetaerae

They lie in their long hair, with brown faces
that have departed deep into themselves.
The eyes closed, as if from too much distance.
Skeletons, mouths, flowers. Inside the mouths
the smooth teeth like a pocket chess set
arrayed in ivory rows.
And flowers, yellow pearls, slender bones,
hands and tunics, faded weaving
above the caved-in heart. But
there beneath those rings, talismans,
and eye-blue stones (cherished keepsakes),
there still stands the silent crypt of the sex,
filled to its vaulted roof with flower petals.
And again yellow pearls, rolled far asunder,
dishes of baked clay, whose shell
their own image once adorned, green shards
of ointment vases that smelled like flowers,
and statues of little gods: household altars,
Hetaerae-heavens with enraptured gods.
Loosened waistbands, flat scarab stones,
small figures with gigantic sexes,
a laughing mouth and dancing girls and messengers,
golden clasps that look like tiny bows
for hunting beast- and bird-shaped amulets,
and long needles, ornamented household things,
a round potsherd made of reddish earth,
and on it, like an entranceway's dark inscription,
the tense legs of a team of horses.
And again flowers, pearls that have come unstrung,

the bright loins of a small lyre,
and between veils that fall like mist,
as if crept forth the shoe's chrysalis:
the ankle's pale butterfly.

And so they lie filled up with things,
precious things, jewels, toys, bowls and spoons,
broken trifles (all that was tossed into them),
and grow dark like the bottom of a river.

And they *were* riverbeds,
over whom in brief, rapid waves
(all pressing onward to the next life)
the bodies of many young men plunged,
and in whom grown men's torrents roared.
And sometimes boys would break out of the mountains
of childhood, descend in timid falls
and play with the things on the bottom
until the slope gripped their feelings:

Then they filled the whole breadth of that
wide course with clear, shallow water,
and started eddies running in the deeper places,
and mirrored for the first time the banks
and the distant call of birds—, while high above
the starry nights of a sweet country
blossomed into heavens that nowhere closed.

YANNOS RITSOS

Translated from the Greek by Edmund Keeley

Miniature

The woman stood up in front of the table. Her sad hands
begin to cut thin slices of lemon for tea
like yellow wheels for a very small carriage
made for a child's fairy tale. The young officer sitting opposite
is buried in the old armchair. He doesn't look at her.
He lights up his cigarette. His hand holding the match trembles,
throwing light on his tender chin and the teacup's handle. The
   clock
holds its heartbeat for a moment. Something has been postponed.
The moment has gone. It's too late now. Let's drink our tea.
Is it possible, then, for death to come in that kind of carriage?
To pass by and go away? And only this carriage to remain,
with its little yellow wheels of lemon
parked for so many years on a side street with unlit lamps,
and then a small song, a little mist, and then nothing?

Dolor

I have known the inexorable sadness of pencils,
Neat in their boxes, dolor of pad and paper-weight,
All the misery of manilla folders and mucilage,
Desolation in immaculate public places,
Lonely reception room, lavatory, switchboard,
The unalterable pathos of basin and pitcher,
Ritual of multigraph, paper-clip, comma,
Endless duplication of lives and objects.
And I have seen dust from the walls of institutions,
Finer than flour, alive, more dangerous than silica,
Sift, almost invisible, through long afternoons of tedium,
Dropping a fine film on nails and delicate eyebrows,
Glazing the pale hair, the duplicate grey standard faces.

TADEUSZ ROZEWICZ
Translated from the Polish by Joanna Trzeciak

In the Middle of Life

After the end of the world
after my death
I found myself in the middle of life
creating myself
building a life
people animals landscapes

this is a tablet I kept saying
this is a table
on the table are the bread the knife
the knife is used for cutting bread
people feed on bread

man should be loved
I learned by night by day
what should one love
I answered man

this is a window I kept saying
this is a window
beyond the window is a garden
in the garden I see an apple tree
the apple tree blossoms
the blossoms fall off
fruit forms
ripens

my father picks an apple
the man picking the apple
is my father

I was sitting on the front steps of the house
that old woman
pulling a goat on a rope
is more needed
is worth more
than the seven wonders of the world
anyone who thinks or feels
she isn't needed
is guilty of genocide

this is a man
this is a tree this is bread
people eat in order to live
I kept repeating to myself
human life is important
human life has great importance
the value of life
surpasses the value of every object
man has made
man is a great treasure
I kept repeating stubbornly

this is water I kept saying
stroking the waves with my hand
talking to the river
water I said
kind water
it is I

the man talked to the water
talked to the moon
to the flowers to the rain
he talked to the earth
to the birds
to the sky

the sky was silent
the earth was silent
if he heard a voice
flowing
from the earth the water the sky
it was the voice of another man

GEORGE SEFERIS

Translated from the Greek by Edmund Keeley and Philip Sherrard

Epiphany, 1937

The flowering sea and the mountains in the moon's waning
the great stone close to the Barbary figs and the asphodels
the jar that refused to go dry at the end of day
and the closed bed by the cypress trees and your hair
golden; the stars of the Swan and that other star, Aldebaran.

I've kept a hold on my life, kept a hold on my life, traveling
among yellow trees in driving rain
on silent slopes loaded with beech leaves
no fire on their peaks; it's getting dark.
I've kept a hold on my life; on your left hand a line
a scar at your knee, perhaps they exist
on the sand of the past summer perhaps
they remain there where the north wind blew as I hear
an alien voice around the frozen lake.
The faces I see do not ask questions nor does the woman
bent as she walks giving her child the breast.
I climb the mountains; dark ravines; the snow-covered
plain, into the distance stretches the snow-covered plain,
   they ask nothing
neither time to shut up in dumb chapels nor
hands outstretched to beg, nor the roads.
I've kept a hold on my life whispering in a boundless silence
I no longer know how to speak nor how to think; whispers
like the breathing of the cypress tree that night
like the human voice of the night sea on pebbles
like the memory of your voice saying "happiness."
I close my eyes looking for the secret meeting place of the waters

under the ice the sea's smile, the closed wells
groping with my veins for those veins that escape me
there where the water-lilies end and that man
who walks blindly across the snows of silence.
I've kept a hold on my life, with him, looking for the water that
    touches you
heavy drops on green leaves, on your face
in the empty garden, drops in the motionless reservoir
striking a swan dead in its white wings
living trees and your eyes staring.

This road has no end, has no relief, however hard you try
to recall your childhood years, those who left, those
lost in sleep, in the graves of the sea,
however much you ask bodies you've loved to stoop
under the harsh branches of the plane-trees there
where a ray of the sun, naked, stood still
and a dog leapt and your heart shuddered,
the road has no relief; I've kept a hold on my life.

                                        The snow
and the water frozen in the hoofmarks of the horses.

April Inventory

The green catalpa tree has turned
All white; the cherry blooms once more.
In one whole year I haven't learned
A blessed thing they pay you for.
The blossoms snow down in my hair;
The trees and I will soon be bare.

The trees have more than I to spare.
The sleek, expensive girls I teach,
Younger and pinker every year,
Bloom gradually out of reach.
The pear tree lets its petals drop
Like dandruff on a tabletop.

The girls have grown so young by now
I have to nudge myself to stare.
This year they smile and mind me how
My teeth are falling with my hair.
In thirty years I may not get
Younger, shrewder, or out of debt.

The tenth time, just a year ago,
I made myself a little list
Of all the things I'd ought to know,
Then told my parents, analyst,
And everyone who's trusted me
I'd be substantial, presently.

I haven't read one book about
A book or memorized one plot.
Or found a mind I did not doubt.
I learned one date. And then forgot.
And one by one the solid scholars
Get the degrees, the jobs, the dollars.

And smile above their starchy collars.
I taught my classes Whitehead's notions;
One lovely girl, a song of Mahler's.
Lacking a source-book or promotions,
I showed one child the colors of
A luna moth and how to love.

I taught myself to name my name,
To bark back, loosen love and crying;
To ease my woman so she came,
To ease an old man who was dying.
I have not learned how often I
Can win, can love, but choose to die.

I have not learned there is a lie
Love shall be blonder, slimmer, younger;
That my equivocating eye
Loves only by my body's hunger;
That I have forces, true to feel,
Or that the lovely world is real.

While scholars speak authority
And wear their ulcers on their sleeves,
My eyes in spectacles shall see
These trees procure and spend their leaves.
There is a value underneath
The gold and silver in my teeth.

Though trees turn bare and girls turn wives,
We shall afford our costly seasons;
There is a gentleness survives
That will outspeak and has its reasons.
There is a loveliness exists,
Preserves us, not for specialists.

A Postcard from the Volcano

Children picking up our bones
Will never know that these were once
As quick as foxes on the hill;

And that in autumn, when the grapes
Made sharp air sharper by their smell
These had a being, breathing frost;

And least will guess that with our bones
We left much more, left what still is
The look of things, left what we felt

At what we saw. The spring clouds blow
Above the shuttered mansion-house,
Beyond our gate and the windy sky

Cries out a literate despair.
We knew for long the mansion's look
And what we said of it became

A part of what it is . . . Children,
Still weaving budded aureoles,
Will speak our speech and never know,

Will say of the mansion that it seems
As if he that lived there left behind
A spirit storming in blank walls,

A dirty house in a gutted world,
A tatter of shadows peaked to white,
Smeared with the gold of the opulent sun.

That Winter

In Chicago, near the lake, on the North Shore
your shotgun apartment has a sun room
where you indulge in a cheap
chaise lounge—
and read *Of Human Bondage*—
There is a window in the living-room proper
cracked open so your
Persian cat can go outside.
You are on the first floor and upstairs
a loud-mouthed southern woman,
whose husband is away
all week on business trips,
has brought her maid
up from Georgia
to do the work and take care of the baby.
"O Lord," the southern woman says,
"he wants it spotless on the weekend—"
The maid, who has
smooth brown skin,
is not allowed to sit on the toilet
but she feeds the kid
and changes the dirty diapers.
She washes the dishes,
she cooks the southern meals,
she irons the sheets for the mahogany bed.
The southern woman shouts
at her in a southern drawl,
"Junie, don't sit on that chair

you'll bust it."
The southern woman is at
loose ends five days
waiting for him to come in.
"It's like a honeymoon,
honey," she says—
"When he grabs me,
whooee."
She invites you up and makes
sure you understand
the fine points of being a white woman.
"I can't let her live
here—not in Chicago.
I made her go out
and get herself a room.
She's seventeen.
She bellered and blubbered.
Now I don't know
What she's trackin' in
from men."
It is winter. The ice
stacks up around the
retaining wall—
the lake slaps over
the park benches,
blocks of ice green with algae.
You are getting your mail secretly at a postal box
because your lover is in the Aleutians.

It's during the war and
your disgusting husband
works at an oil refinery
on the South Side.
Up there in the Aleutians
they are knocking the gold
teeth out of the dead Japanese.
One construction worker
has a skin bag with fifty
gold-filled teeth.
He pours them out at
night in his Quonset hut.
He brags about bashing their faces in.
One day you are fooling
around in a downtown music store
waiting for the war to end.
You let a strange teenage boy
talk you into going
home with him.
He lives alone in a basement behind a
square of buildings.
He shows you his knife collection
and talks obsessively about Raskolnikov—suddenly
your genes want to live
and you pull away
and get out of there.
It is almost dusk.
You run until you find the boulevard
sluggish with the 1943 traffic.

You know by now there
isn't much to live for
except to spite Hitler—
The war is so lurid
that everything else is dull.

JULES SUPERVIELLE

Translated from the French by David Gascoyne

Rain and the Tyrants

I stand and watch the rain
Falling in pools which make
Our grave old planet shine;
The clear rain falling, just the same
As that which fell in Homer's time
And that which dropped in Villon's day
Falling on mother and on child
As on the passive backs of sheep;
Rain saying all it has to say
Again and yet again, and yet
Without the power to make less hard
The wooden heads of tyrants or
To soften their stone hearts,
And powerless to make them feel
Amazement as they ought;
A drizzling rain which falls
Across all Europe's map,
Wrapping all men alive
In the same moist envelope;
Despite the soldiers loading arms,
Despite the newspapers' alarms,
Despite all this, all that,
A shower of drizzling rain
Making the flags hang wet.

MAY SWENSON

Question

Body my house
my horse my hound
what will I do
when you are fallen

Where will I sleep
How will I ride
What will I hunt

Where can I go
without my mount
all eager and quick
How will I know
in thicket ahead
is danger or treasure
when Body my good
bright dog is dead

How will it be
to lie in the sky
without roof or door
and wind for an eye

With cloud for shift
how will I hide?

WISŁAWA SZYMBORSKA

Translated from the Polish by Joanna Trzeciak

The End and the Beginning

After every war
someone has to clean up.
Things won't
straighten themselves up, after all.

Someone has to push the rubble
to the side of the road,
so the corpse-filled wagons
can pass.

Someone has to wade through
scum and ashes,
through sofa springs,
splintered glass,
and bloody rags.

Someone has to drag in a girder
to prop up a wall,
someone has to glaze a window,
rehang a door.

Photogenic it's not,
and takes years.
All the cameras have left
for another war.

We'll need the bridges back,
and new railway stations.
Sleeves will go ragged
from rolling them up.

Someone, broom in hand,
still recalls the way it was.
Someone else listens
and nods with unsevered head.
But already there are those nearby
starting to mill about
who will find it dull.

From out of the bushes
sometimes someone still digs up
rust-eaten arguments
and carries them to the garbage pile.

Those who knew
what was going on here
must make way for
those who know little.
And less than little.
And finally as little as nothing.

In the grass that has overgrown
causes and effects,
someone must stretch out
blade of grass in his mouth
gazing at clouds.

Fern Hill

Now as I was young and easy under the apple boughs
About the lilting house and happy as the grass was green,
    The night above the dingle starry,
        Time let me hail and climb
    Golden in the heydays of his eyes,
And honoured among wagons I was prince of the apple towns
And once below a time I lordly had the trees and leaves
        Trail with daisies and barley
    Down the rivers of the windfall light.

And as I was green and carefree, famous among the barns
About the happy yard and singing as the farm was home,
    In the sun that is young once only,
        Time let me play and be
    Golden in the mercy of his means,
And green and golden I was huntsman and herdsman, the calves
Sang to my horn, the foxes on the hills barked clear and cold,
        And the sabbath rang slowly
    In the pebbles of the holy streams.

All the sun long it was running, it was lovely, the hay
Fields high as the house, the tunes from the chimneys, it was air
    And playing, lovely and watery
        And fire green as grass.
    And nightly under the simple stars
As I rode to sleep the owls were bearing the farm away,
All the moon long I heard, blessed among stables, the nightjars
    Flying with the ricks, and the horses
        Flashing into the dark.

And then to awake, and the farm, like a wanderer white
With the dew, come back, the cock on his shoulder: it was all
    Shining, it was Adam and maiden,
        The sky gathered again
    And the sun grew round that very day.
So it must have been after the birth of the simple light
In the first, spinning place, the spellbound horses walking warm
    Out of the whinnying green stable
        On to the fields of praise.

And honoured among foxes and pheasants by the gay house
Under the new made clouds and happy as the heart was long,
    In the sun born over and over,
        I ran my heedless ways,
    My wishes raced through the house high hay
And nothing I cared, at my sky blue trades, that time allows
In all his tuneful turning so few and such morning songs
    Before the children green and golden
        Follow him out of grace,

Nothing I cared, in the lamb white days, that time would take me
Up to the swallow thronged loft by the shadow of my hand,
    In the moon that is always rising,
        Nor that riding to sleep
    I should hear him fly with the high fields
And wake to the farm forever fled from the childless land.
Oh as I was young and easy in the mercy of his means,
        Time held me green and dying
    Though I sang in my chains like the sea.

Rain

Rain, midnight rain, nothing but the wild rain
On this bleak hut, and solitude, and me
Remembering again that I shall die
And neither hear the rain nor give it thanks
For washing me cleaner than I have been
Since I was born into this solitude.
Blessed are the dead that the rain rains upon:
But here I pray that none whom once I loved
Is dying to-night or lying still awake
Solitary, listening to the rain,
Either in pain or thus in sympathy
Helpless among the living and the dead,
Like a cold water among broken reeds,
Myriads of broken reeds all still and stiff,
Like me who have no love which this wild rain
Has not dissolved except the love of death,
If love it be for what is perfect and
Cannot, the tempest tells me, disappoint.

TOMAS TRANSTRÖMER

Translated from the Swedish by Robert Bly

Track

2 a.m.: moonlight. The train has stopped
out in a field. Far off sparks of light from a town,
flickering coldly on the horizon.

As when a man goes so deep into his dream
he will never remember that he was there
when he returns again to his room.

Or when a person goes so deep into a sickness
that his days all become some flickering sparks, a swarm,
feeble and cold on the horizon.

The train is entirely motionless.
2 o'clock: strong moonlight, few stars.

MARINA TSVETAEVA

Translated from the Russian by Elaine Feinstein

An Attempt at Jealousy

How is your life with the other one,
Simpler, isn't it? One stroke of the oar
Then a long coastline, and soon
Even the memory of me

Will be a floating island
(In the sky, not on the waters):
Spirits, spirits, you will be
Sisters, and never lovers.

How is your life with an ordinary
Woman? without godhead?
Now that your sovereign has
Been deposed (and you have stepped down),

How is your life? Are you fussing?
Flinching? How do you get up?
The tax of deathless vulgarity,
Can you cope with it, poor man?

"Scenes and hysterics—I've had
Enough! I'll rent my own house."
How is your life with the other one
Now, you that I chose for my own?

More to your taste, more delicious
Is it, your food? Don't moan if you sicken.
How is your life with an *image*,
You, who walked on Sinai?

How is your life with a stranger
From this world? Can you (be frank)
Love her? Or do you feel shame
Like Zeus's reins on your forehead?

How is your life? Are you
Healthy? How do you sing?
How do you deal with the pain
Of an undying conscience, poor man?

How is your life with a piece of market
Stuff, at a steep price?
After Carrara marble,
How is your life with the dust of

Plaster now? (God was hewn from
Stone, but he is smashed to bits.)
How do you live with one of a
Thousand women, after Lilith?

Sated with newness, are you?
Now you are grown cold to magic,
How is your life with an
Earthly woman, without a sixth

Sense? Tell me: are you happy?
Not? In a shallow pit? How is
Your life, my love? Is it as
Hard as mine with another man?

XAVIER VILLAURRUTIA
Translated from the Spanish by Donald Justice

Rose Nocturnal

to José Gorostiza

I too speak of the rose.
But my rose is neither the cold rose
nor the one in a child's skin,
nor the rose which turns
so slowly that its motion
is a mysterious form of stillness.

It is not the thirsty rose,
nor the wound bleeding,
nor the rose crowned with thorns,
nor the rose of the resurrection.

It is not the rose with naked petals,
nor the wax rose,
nor the silken flame,
nor yet the quick-blushing rose.

It is not the banner rose,
nor the secret garden-rot,
nor the punctual rose telling the hour,
nor the compass rose of the mariner.

No, it is not the rose rose
but the uncreated rose,
the rose submerged,
the nocturnal,
the unsubstantial rose,
the void rose.

It is the rose of touch in darkness,
it is the rose that comes forward inflamed,
the rose of rosy nails,
the bud rose of eager fingertips,
the digital rose,
the blind rose.

It is the molded rose of hearing,
the ear rose,
the noise's spiral,
the shell rose always left behind
in the loudest surf of the pillow.

It is the fleshed rose of the mouth,
the rose that, waking, speaks
as though it were sleeping.
It is the half-open rose
from out of which pours shade,
the entrail rose
that folds up and expands,
required, desired, devoured,
it is the labial rose,
the wounded rose.

It is the rose that opens its lids,
the vigilant, wakeful rose,
the shattered rose of insomnia.

It is the rose of smoke,
the ash rose,
the diamond coal's black rose
which, noiseless, drills through darkness
and occupies no point in space.

DEREK WALCOTT

The Season of Phantasmal Peace

Then all the nations of birds lifted together
the huge net of the shadows of this earth
in multitudinous dialects, twittering tongues,
stitching and crossing it. They lifted up
the shadows of long pines down trackless slopes,
the shadows of glass-faced towers down, evening streets,
the shadow of a frail plant on a city sill—
the net rising soundless as night, the birds' cries soundless, until
there was no longer dusk, or season, decline, or weather,
only this passage of phantasmal light
that not the narrowest shadow dared to sever.

And men could not see, looking up, what the wild geese drew,
what the ospreys trailed behind them in silvery ropes
that flashed in the icy sunlight; they could not hear
battalions of starlings waging peaceful cries,
bearing the net higher, covering this world
like the vines of an orchard, or a mother drawing
the trembling gauze over the trembling eyes
of a child fluttering to sleep;
                                    it was the light
that you will see at evening on the side of a hill
in yellow October, and no one hearing knew
what change had brought into the raven's cawing,
the killdeer's screech, the ember-circling chough
such an immense, soundless, and high concern
for the fields and cities where the birds belong,
except it was their seasonal passing, Love,
made seasonless, or, from the high privilege of their birth,

something brighter than pity for the wingless ones
below them who shared dark holes in windows and in houses,
and higher they lifted the net with soundless voices
above all change, betrayals of falling suns,
and this season lasted one moment, like the pause
between dusk and darkness, between fury and peace,
but, for such as our earth is now, it lasted long.

Lullaby: Moonlight Lingers

Moonlight lingers down the air.
Moonlight marks the window-square
As I stand and watch you sleep.
I hear the rustle where
The sea stirs sweet and sighs in its silvered sleep.
My son, sleep deep.
Sleep deep, son, and dream how moonlight
Unremitting, whitely, whitely, unpetals down the night.
As you sleep, now moonlight
Mollifies the mountain's rigor,
Laves the olive leaf to silver,
And black on the moon-pale trunk of the olive
Prints the shadow of an olive leaf.
Sleep, let moonlight give
That dark secondary definition to the olive leaf.
Sleep, son, past grief.

Now I close my eyes and see
Moonlight white on a certain tree.
It was a big white oak near a door
Familiar, long back, to me,
But now years unseen, and my foot enters there no more.
My son, sleep deep.
Sleep deep, son, and let me think
How a summer lane glimmers in moonlight to the cedar woods'
    dark brink.
Sleep, and let me now think
Of moon-frost white on the black boughs of cedar,
White moon-rinse on meadow, whiter than clover,

And at moon-dark stone, how water woke
In a wink of glory, then slid on to sleep.
Sleep, let this moon provoke
Moonlight more white on that landscape lost in the heart's homely
    deep.
Son, past grief, sleep.

Moonlight falls on sleeping faces.
It fell in far times and other places.
Moonlight falls on your face now,
And now in memory's stasis
I see moonlight mend an old man's Time-crossed brow.
My son, sleep deep,
For moonlight will not stay.
Now moves to seek that empty pillow, a hemisphere away.
Here, then, you'll be waking to the day.
Those who died, died long ago,
Faces you will never know,
Voices you will never hear—
Though your father heard them in the night,
And yet, sometimes, I can hear
Their utterance like the rustling tongue of a pale tide in moon-
    light:
Sleep, son, Good night.

Advice to a Prophet

When you come, as you soon must, to the streets of our city,
Mad-eyed from stating the obvious,
Not proclaiming our fall but begging us
In God's name to have self-pity,

Spare us all word of the weapons, their force and range,
The long numbers that rocket the mind;
Our slow, unreckoning hearts will be left behind,
Unable to fear what is too strange.

Nor shall you scare us with talk of the death of the race.
How should we dream of this place without us?—
The sun mere fire, the leaves untroubled about us,
A stone look on the stone's face?

Speak of the world's own change. Though we cannot conceive
Of an undreamt thing, we know to our cost
How the dreamt cloud crumbles, the vines are blackened by frost,
How the view alters. We could believe,

If you told us so, that the white-tailed deer will slip
Into perfect shade, grown perfectly shy,
The lark avoid the reaches of our eye,
The jack-pine lose its knuckled grip

On the cold ledge, and every torrent burn
As Xanthus once, its gliding trout
Stunned in a twinkling. What should we be without
The dolphin's arc, the dove's return,

These things in which we have seen ourselves and spoken?
Ask us, prophet, how we shall call
Our natures forth when that live tongue is all
Dispelled, that glass obscured or broken

In which we have said the rose of our love and the clean
Horse of our courage, in which beheld
The singing locust of the soul unshelled,
And all we mean or wish to mean.

Ask us, ask us whether with the worldless rose
Our hearts shall fail us; come demanding
Whether there shall be lofty or long standing
When the bronze annals of the oak-tree close.

These

are the desolate, dark weeks
when nature in its barrenness
equals the stupidity of man.

The year plunges into night
and the heart plunges
lower than night

to an empty, windswept place
without sun, stars or moon
but a peculiar light as of thought

that spins a dark fire—
whirling upon itself until,
in the cold, it kindles

to make a man aware of nothing
that he knows, not loneliness
itself—Not a ghost but

would be embraced—emptiness,
despair—(They
whine and whistle) among

the flashes and booms of war;
houses of whose rooms
the cold is greater than can be thought,

the people gone that we loved,
the beds lying empty, the couches
damp, the chairs unused—

Hide it away somewhere
out of the mind, let it get roots
and grow, unrelated to jealous

ears and eyes—for itself.
In this mine they come to dig—all.
Is this the counterfoil to sweetest

music? The source of poetry that
seeing the clock stopped, says,
The clock has stopped

that ticked yesterday so well?
and hears the sound of lakewater
splashing—that is now stone.

JAMES WRIGHT

The Journey

Anghiari is medieval, a sleeve sloping down
A steep hill, suddenly sweeping out
To the edge of a cliff, and dwindling.
But far up the mountain, behind the town,
We too were swept out, out by the wind,
Alone with the Tuscan grass.

Wind had been blowing across the hills
For days, and everything now was graying gold
With dust, everything we saw, even
Some small children scampering along a road,
Twittering Italian to a small caged bird.

We sat beside them to rest in some brushwood,
And I leaned down to rinse the dust from my face.

I found the spider web there, whose hinges
Reeled heavily and crazily with the dust,
Whole mounds and cemeteries of it, sagging
And scattering shadows among shells and wings.
And then she stepped into the center of air
Slender and fastidious, the golden hair
Of daylight along her shoulders, she poised there,
While ruins crumbled on every side of her.
Free of the dust, as though a moment before
She had stepped inside the earth, to bathe herself.

I gazed, close to her, till at last she stepped
Away in her own good time.

Many men
Have searched all over Tuscany and never found
What I found there, the heart of the light
Itself shelled and leaved, balancing
On filaments themselves falling. The secret
Of this journey is to let the wind
Blow its dust all over your body,
To let it go on blowing, to step lightly, lightly
All the way through your ruins, and not to lose
Any sleep over the dead, who surely
Will bury their own, don't worry.

RICHARD WRIGHT

I Have Seen Black Hands

I am black and I have seen black hands, millions and millions of
  them—
Out of millions of bundles of wool and flannel tiny black fingers
  have reached restlessly and hungrily for life.
Reached out for the black nipples at the black breasts of black
  mothers,
And they've held red, green, blue, yellow, orange, white, and purple
  toys in the childish grips of possession,
And chocolate drops, peppermint sticks, lollypops, wineballs, ice
  cream cones, and sugared cookies in fingers sticky and gummy,
And they've held balls and bats and gloves and marbles and jack-
  knives and slingshots and spinning tops in the thrill of sport and
  play,
And pennies and nickels and dimes and quarters and sometimes on
  New Year's, Easter, Lincoln's Birthday, May Day, a brand new
  green dollar bill,
They've held pens and rulers and maps and tablets and books in
  palms spotted and smeared with ink,
And they've held dice and cards and half-pint flasks and cue sticks
  and cigars and cigarettes in the pride of new maturity . . .

II

I am black and I have seen black hands, millions and millions of
  them—
They were tired and awkward and calloused and grimy and covered
  with hangnails,

And they were caught in the fast-moving belts of machines and
   snagged and smashed and crushed,
And they jerked up and down at the throbbing machines massing
   taller and taller the heaps of gold in the banks of bosses,
And they piled higher and higher the steel, iron, the lumber, wheat,
   rye, the oats, corn, the cotton, the wool, the oil, the coat, the
   meat, the fruit, the glass, and the stone until there was too much
   to be used,
And they grabbed guns and slung them on their shoulders and
   marched and groped in trenches and fought and killed and
   conquered nations who were customers for the goods black
   hands made.
And again black hands stacked goods higher and higher until there
   was too much to be used,
And then the black hands held trembling at the factory gates the
   dreaded lay-off slip,
And the black hands hung idle and swung empty and grew soft and
   got weak and bony from unemployment and starvation,
And they grew nervous and sweaty, and opened and shut in anguish
   and doubt and hesitation and irresolution . . .

III

I am black and I have seen black hands, millions and millions of
   them—
Reaching hesitantly out of days of slow death for the goods they
   had made, but the bosses warned that the goods were private and
   did not belong to them,

And the black hands struck desperately out in defence of life and
   there was blood, but the enraged bosses decreed that this too
   was wrong,
And the black hands felt the cold steel bars of the prison they had
   made, in despair tested their strength and found that they could
   neither bend nor break them,
And the black hands fought and scratched and held back but a
   thousand white hands took them and tied them,
And the black hands lifted palms in mute and futile supplication to
   the sodden faces of mobs wild in the revelries of sadism,
And the black hands strained and clawed and struggled in vain at
   the noose that tightened about the black throat,
And the black hands waved and beat fearfully at the tall flames that
   cooked and charred the black flesh . . .

   IV

I am black and I have seen black hands
Raised in fists of revolt, side by side with the white fists of white
   workers,
And some day—and it is only this which sustains me—
Some day there shall be millions and millions of them,
On some red day in a burst of fists on a new horizon!

WILLIAM BUTLER YEATS

In Memory of Eva Gore-Booth and Con Markievicz

The light of evening, Lissadell,
Great windows open to the south,
Two girls in silk kimonos, both
Beautiful, one a gazelle.
But a raving autumn shears
Blossom from the summer's wreath;
The older is condemned to death,
Pardoned, drags out lonely years
Conspiring among the ignorant.
I know not what the younger dreams—
Some vague Utopia—and she seems,
When withered old and skeleton-gaunt,
An image of such politics.
Many a time I think to seek
One or the other out and speak
Of that old Georgian mansion, mix
Pictures of the mind, recall
That table and the talk of youth,
Two girls in silk kimonos, both
Beautiful, one a gazelle.

Dear shadows, now you know it all,
All the folly of a fight
With a common wrong or right.
The innocent and the beautiful
Have no enemy but time;
Arise and bid me strike a match
And strike another till time catch;

Should the conflagration climb,
Run till all the sages know.
We the great gazebo built,
They convicted us of guilt;
Bid me strike a match and blow.

October 1927

ANDREA ZANZOTTO
Translated from the Italian by Ruth Feldman and Brian Swann

That's How We Are

They said, the friends at Padua,
"I knew him too."
And there was nearby the rumble of dirty water,
and of a dirty factory:
stupendous in the silence.
Because it was night. "I
knew him too."
Keenly I thought
of you who now
are neither subject nor object
not usual speech nor jargon
not quiet nor motion
not even the not that negated—
and for all that my eyes
pierce its needle eye—
never negates you enough

So be it: but I believe
with equal force
in all my nothingness,
therefore I haven't lost you
or, the more I lose you and you lose yourself,
the more like me you are, the closer you come.

"A"-11

for Celia and Paul

River that must turn full after I stop dying
Song, my song, raise grief to music
Light as my loves' thought, the few sick
So sick of wrangling: thus weeping,
Sounds of light, stay in her keeping
And my son's face—this much for honor.

Freed by their praises who make honor dearer
Whose losses show them rich and you no poorer
Take care, song, that what stars' imprint you mirror
Grazes their tears; draw speech from their nature or
Love in you—faced to your outer stars—purer
Gold than tongues make without feeling
Art new, hurt old: revealing
The slackened bow as the stinging
Animal dies, thread gold stringing
The fingerboard pressed in my honor.

Honor, song, sang the blest is delight knowing
We overcome ills by love. Hurt, song, nourish
Eyes, think most of whom you hurt. For the flowing
River's poison where what rod blossoms. Flourish
By love's sweet lights and sing *in them I flourish.*
No, song, not any one power
May recall or forget, our
Love to see your love flows into
Us. If Venus lights, your words spin, to
Live our desires lead us to honor.

Graced, your heart in nothing less than in death, go—
I, dust—raise the great hem of the extended
World that nothing can leave; having had breath go
Face my son, say: "If your father offended
You with mute wisdom, my words have not ended
His second paradise where
His love was in her eyes where
They turn, quick for you two—sick
Or gone cannot make music
You set less than all. Honor

His voice in me, the river's turn that finds the
Grace in you, four notes first too full for talk, leaf
Lighting stem, stems bound to the branch that binds the
Tree, and then as from the same root we talk, leaf
After leaf of your mind's music, page, walk leaf
Over leaf of his thought, sounding
His happiness: song sounding
The grace that comes from knowing
Things, her love our own showing
Her love in all her honor."

Biographies

Anna Andreyevna Akhmatova (1889–1966) was born Anna Gorenko in Odessa, the Ukraine. The celebrated, politically controversial author of numerous volumes of poetry—*Vecher, Chyotki, Belaya staya, Podorozhnik, Anno Domini MCMXXI*, and the posthumously published long poem "Poema bez geroya"—she also translated Hugo, Tagore, and Leopardi and wrote memoirs of Blok, Modigliani, and Mandelstam. Akhmatova became president of the Writers' Union and was awarded the Etna-Taormina prize in 1964. She died in St. Petersburg.

Rafael Alberti (1902–1999) was born in El Puerto de Santa Maria. In 1917 his family moved to Madrid, where he studied painting. He started to write in 1921 while recovering from tuberculosis, which had prevented him from painting; his first book, *Marinero en Tierra*, won the National Prize for Literature. Thereafter he published numerous poetry volumes, including *Cal y Canto, Sobre los Angeles*, and *Poesías Completas*, as well as essays about art. Alberti lived in exile in France, Argentina, and Italy.

Yehuda Amichai (1924–2000) was born in Würzburg, Germany, and moved to Jerusalem with his family when he was thirteen, later becoming a naturalized Israeli citizen. His first language was German, but he read Hebrew fluently and studied the Bible and Hebrew literature at university. In World War II he fought with the Jewish Brigade of the British Army. His first book, *Achshav Uve-Yamim HaAharim*, appeared in 1955. He published ten further collections of poems, two novels, and a collection of short stories, and his work has been translated into nearly forty languages. Amichai received the Shlonsky Prize, a pair of Acum Prizes, the Bialik Prize, and the Israeli Prize for Poetry.

Archie Randolph Ammons (1926–2001) was born in Whiteville, North Carolina. He published nearly thirty volumes of poetry, including *Glare, Garbage, A Coast of Trees, Sphere, Tape for the Turn of the Year, Expressions at Sea Level*, and *Corsons Inlet*, and his honors included two National Book Awards, the Bollingen Prize, the National Book Critics Circle Award, the Academy of American Poets' Tanning Prize, and a MacArthur Foundation fellowship.

Carlos Drummond de Andrade (1902–1987) was born in Itabira, in the Brazilian state of Minas Gerais. He began a modernist literary journal, earned a degree in pharmacology, and worked in the Department of Education. He published his first book of poetry, *Alguma Poesia*, in 1930, and his many subsequent volumes include *Brejo das Almas*, *Sentimento do Mundo*, *José*, *A Rosa do Povo*, *Claro Enigma*, *A Vida Passado a Limpo*, and *A Paixão Medida*. He died in Rio de Janeiro.

Mário Raul de Morais de Andrade (1893–1945), one of the founders of modernism in Brazil, was born in São Paulo. He argued for independence from Portugal. Having studied music, drama, anthropology, and folklore, Andrade wrote literary and art criticism, as well as several studies of music, including *Ensayo sobre la música brasileña* and *La música y las canciones populares de Brasil*. From 1935 on, he served as director of São Paulo's department of culture. Andrade also wrote fiction and poetry, the latter going unpublished until a decade after his death.

According to a biographical note, American writer **Alan Ansen** "believes that a man's private life should remain private except as it may be revealed by his works." His first collection, *The Old Religion*, was printed in limited edition by the Tibor de Nagy Gallery. After the appearance of his first commercial volume, *Disorderly Houses*, his work was available only in self-made editions, until *Contact Highs: Selected Poems 1957–1987* brought him back to wider attention. He served as W. H. Auden's secretary, resulting in a volume of conversations, *The Table Talk of W. H. Auden*. Ansen has personal and artistic links to the Beat and the New York School poets.

Guillaume Apollinaire (1880–1918) was born Wilhelm-Apollinaris de Kostrowitzky in Rome and grew up in Monaco, Paris, Cannes, and Nice. As a youngster he adopted the identity of a Russian prince, was once detained on suspicion of having stolen *The Mona Lisa*, and served in World War I. His poetry volumes—by turns symbolist, cubist, and surrealist—include *L'enchanteur pourrissant*, *Le Bestiaire*, *Vitam Impendere Amori*, *Alcools*, *Le poète assassiné*, and the posthumously published concrete poems *Calligrammes: poèmes de la paix et de la guerre*. Apollinaire also wrote fiction, drama, screenplays, pornography, and criticism. His play *Les Mamelles de Tirésias* became the subject of an opera by Poulenc, while *L'esprit nouveau et les poëtes* articulates his aesthetic and political views.

Born in Rochester, New York, in 1927, **John Ashbery** is the author of twenty individual volumes of poetry, most recently *Chinese Whispers* and *Your Name Here*, as well as several books of criticism, fiction, and drama. In

1976 his *Self-Portrait in a Convex Mirror* won the Pulitzer Prize, the National Book Award, and the National Book Critics Circle Award. He has been Charles Eliot Norton Lecturer in Poetry at Harvard, a MacArthur fellow and twice a Guggenheim fellow, and winner of the Bollingen and Lenore Marshall/*Nation* poetry prizes.

Wystan Hugh Auden (1907–1973) was born in York, England, and studied at Oxford. After serving in the Spanish Civil War, he moved to the United States in 1939 and became an American citizen. His numerous poetry books include *The Orators*; *Look, Stranger!*; *Spain*; *The Sea and the Mirror*; *The Age of Anxiety*; *Nones*; *The Shield of Achilles*; *The Old Man's Road*; *Homage to Clio*; *About the House*; *City without Walls*; *Academic Graffiti*; *Epistle to a Godson*; and *Thank You, Fog*. Auden wrote plays, libretti, and criticism such as *The Dyer's Hand* and *Forewords and Afterwords*. He judged the Yale Series of Younger Poets for many years.

Ingeborg Bachmann (1926–1973) was born in Klagenfurt, Austria. A student of philosophy, she wrote her dissertation on Heidegger. The author of two poetry volumes, she won the poetry prize from Gruppe 47 for her first, *Die gestundete Zeit*, followed three years later by *Anrufung des Großen Bären*. She also wrote a novel, short stories, essays, radio drama, and opera libretti, as well as translating Akhmatova and Ungaretti. Her honors included the Georg Büchner Prize, the Berlin Critics Prize, the Bremen Award, and the Austrian State Prize for Literature. She died in Rome, having lived in Munich and Zurich.

John Berryman (1914–1972) was born John Allyn Smith Jr. in McAlester, Oklahoma. His book *77 Dream Songs* was awarded the Pulitzer Prize, before being continued in *His Toy, His Dream, His Rest*—winner of the National Book Award and the Bollingen Prize—completing *The Dream Songs*. Berryman's other volumes include *Poems*; *The Dispossessed*; *Homage to Mistress Bradstreet*; *Berryman's Sonnets*; *Love & Fame*; and *Delusions, Etc.*

Elizabeth Bishop (1911–1979) authored four volumes of poetry—*North and South*, *A Cold Spring*, *Questions of Travel*, and *Geography III*—and translated *The Diary of "Helena Morley."* Born in Worcester, Massachusetts, she spent her early childhood in Great Village, Nova Scotia, thereafter living variously in New York, Key West, Europe, and Brazil. She served as poet-in-residence at Harvard in 1969.

Louise Bogan (1897–1970) was born in Livermore Falls, Maine. Her books of poetry include *The Body of This Death*, *Dark Summer*, *The Sleeping Fury*, and *The Blue Estuaries: Poems 1923–1968*. She was a book reviewer for *The New Yorker* for almost four decades, and her criticism has been collected as *Achievement in American Poetry 1900–1950, Selected Criticism,* and *A Poet's Alphabet.*

Jorge Luis Borges (1899–1986) was born in Buenos Aires, Argentina, and educated in Europe. Director of the National Library of Buenos Aires from 1955 to 1973 and Charles Eliot Norton Professor of Poetry at Harvard from 1967 to 1968, he published numerous books of poetry, fiction, and criticism, including *Fervor de Buenos Aires, Historia universal de la infamia, Luna de enfrente, Inquisiciones, El hacedor, Ficciones, El Informe de Brodie,* and *El Aleph.* He shared the International Publishers' Prize with Samuel Beckett in 1961.

Greek poet **Constantine P. Cavafy** (1863–1933) was born in Alexandria, Egypt, and spent his childhood in England and Constantinople. He wrote his first poems in English, French, and Greek. At twenty-nine he took up an appointment as special clerk in the Irrigation Service of the Ministry of Public Works in Egypt, a position he held for thirty years. Cavafy never allowed a volume of his poems to be sold, instead distributing privately folders of his broadsheets and the pamphlets he printed. His first collected edition appeared two years after his death. In 1926 Cavafy received the Order of the Phoenix from Greek dictator Pangalos.

Paul Celan (1920–1970) was born Paul Antschel in Czernovitz, Romania, of German-speaking Jews. He was interned for a year and a half by the Nazis. Having studied medicine in France before the war, afterward he lived in Bucharest and Vienna before settling in Paris to study German philology and literature, taking his Licence des Lettres in 1950. In 1959 he became a reader in German language and literature at L'École Normal Superieure. Celan's poetry volumes are *Der Sand aus den Urnen, Mohn und Gedächtnis, Von Schwelle zu Schwelle, Sprachgitter, Die Niemandsrose, Atemwende, Fadensonnen, Lightzwang, Schneepart,* and *Zeitgehöft.* He translated Rimbaud, Michaux, Char, Valéry, Pessoa, Shakespeare, Dickinson, Mandelstam, and others, and won the Georg Büchner Prize.

Blaise Cendrars (1887–1961) was born Frédéric Louis Sauser at La Chaux-de-Fonds, Neuchâtel, in Switzerland, adopting his pseudonym at age twenty. His books of poetry include *Les Paques à New York, La Prose du Transsibérien et la petite Jehanne de France,* and *Le Panama ou Les Aventures de Mes Sept Oncles.* After fighting in the French Foreign Legion during World War I, he became involved with the interwar French, Italian, and American film industries and dropped poetry altogether in 1925 in favor of writing fiction. He was awarded the Paris Grand Prix for literature in 1961 and died in Paris.

Aimé Césaire was born in 1913 in Basse-Pointe, Martinique, in the French Caribbean, moved to Paris with a scholarship in 1931, and returned to Martinique eight years later. His political career began in 1945, when he was elected mayor of Fort-de-France and deputy in the Première Assemblée Nationale Constituante. He later resigned from the French Communist Party to begin the Parti Progressiste Martiniquais, retiring from politics in 1993. He is credited with starting the concept of "négritude." Césaire's poetry books include *Cahier d'un retour au pays natal*, *Les Armes miraculeuses*, *Soleil cou coupe*, *Corps perdu*, *Ferrements*, *Cadastre*, and *Moi, laminaire*. . . . He has also authored the plays *Et les chiens se taisaient*; *Une Tempete*, a postcolonial version of Shakespeare's *The Tempest*; *La Tragedie du roi Christophe*; and *Une Saison au Congo*.

Inger Christensen was born in 1935 in Vejle, Denmark, and trained as a teacher. Her poetry volumes are *Lys*, *Græs*, *det*, *Brev i april*, *alphabet*, and *Sommerfugledalen—et requiem*. She is also the author of several plays, children's books, two volumes of essays, and the novels *Evighedsmaskinen*, *Azorno*, and *Det malede værelse*. Among her many awards are the Critics' Prize, the Danish Booksellers' Golden Laurels, the Swedish Academy Nordic Prize, Der Österreichische Staatspreis für Literatur, Preis der Stadt Münster für Europäische Poesie, the Grand Prix des Biennales Internationales de Poesie, and a lifetime grant from the Danish Art Foundations.

Amy Clampitt (1920–1994) was born and raised in New Providence, Iowa, and lived most of her adulthood in New York. In 1983, at age sixty-three, she published her first full-length poetry collection, *The Kingfisher*. Her subsequent poetry books include *What the Light Was Like*, *Archaic Figure*, *Westward*, and *A Silence Opens*, as well as a volume of essays, *Predecessors, Et Cetera*. She earned fellowships from the MacArthur and Guggenheim Foundations.

Harold Hart Crane (1899–1932) was born in Garrettsville, Ohio, began writing in his early teens, did not complete high school, and never attended university. He worked variously as a reporter, as an employee in his father's candy factory, and as a copywriter for mail-order catalogs and ad agencies. His poetry volumes are *White Buildings* and the book-length poem *The Bridge*, which won the annual *Poetry* award. He lived in New York City, on the Isle of Pines in the Caribbean, and, with a Guggenheim fellowship, in Mexico. He died by jumping from an ocean liner, somewhere off the Florida coast.

A native of Paris, **Robert Desnos** (1900–1945) was an early practitioner of automatic writing but broke with surrealism in the early 1930s. The author of a dozen poetry books, including *Language cuit*, *Journal d'une apparition*,

Corps et biens, and *Le sans cou*, he wrote a poem each day throughout 1936. During World War II he fought for the French Resistance and wrote essays mocking the Nazis. Imprisoned at Auschwitz and later in Czechoslovakia, Desnos died of typhus after the camp was liberated.

Hilda Doolittle (H.D.) (1886–1961) was born in Bethlehem, Pennsylvania. After university, she went to Europe and remained abroad for the rest of her life. Linked aesthetically to Imagism, politically to feminism, and intellectually to psychoanalysis and mythology, H.D. published numerous volumes of poems, including *Sea Garden*, *The God*, *Hymen*, *Heliodora and Other Poems*, *Hippolytus Temporizes*, *Red Roses From Bronze*, *By Avon River*, and *Hermetic Definition*, as well as the book-length works *Helen in Egypt* and *The Trilogy*. Her prose texts are *Nights*, *Tribute to Freud*, *End to Torment*, and *The Gift*.

Alan Dugan (1923–2003) was born in Brooklyn, New York. His first book, *Poems*, selected for the Yale Series of Younger Poets, won the National Book Award and the Pulitzer Prize. *Poems Seven: New and Complete Poetry*, also won a National Book Award. Dugan received the Levinson Award from *Poetry*, the Prix de Rome from the American Academy of Arts and Letters, and Guggenheim and Rockefeller fellowships.

Robert Duncan (1919–1988), born Edward Howard Duncan in Oakland, California, was raised by a foster family of Theosophists. Politically left-wing, openly homosexual, concerned with the occult, Duncan divided his time among New York City, North Carolina, and San Francisco. His poetry books include *Heavenly City, Earthly City*; *The Opening of the Field*; *Roots and Branches*; *Bending the Bow*; *Ground Work: Before the War*; and *Ground Work II: In the Dark*. He also authored *The Truth and Life of Myth: An Essay in Essential Autobiography* and the serialized *H.D. Book*. He won the National Poetry Award, the Harriet Monroe Memorial Prize, a Guggenheim fellowship, and the Levinson Prize.

Poet, dramatist, critic, and publishing director **Thomas Stearns Eliot** (1888–1965) was born in St. Louis, Missouri. He studied at Harvard, Oxford, and in Germany, and spent his adult life in England, where he directed Faber and Faber. He was the author of, among many other works, the poems *The Waste Land* and *The Four Quartets*; the plays *Murder in the Cathedral*, *The Family Reunion*, and *The Cocktail Party*; literary criticism *The Sacred Wood*, *The Use of Poetry and the Use of Criticism*, and *On Poetry and Poets*; and the social critique *Notes Towards the Definition of Culture*. He received the Nobel Prize for Literature in 1948.

Odysseus Elytis (1911–1996) was born Odysseus Alepoudhelis in Heraklion, Crete. After studying law and serving as a second lieutenant in

World War II, he traveled frequently, to France, Italy, Switzerland, the United States, the Soviet Union, and Bulgaria, often representing Greece at cultural congresses. At home he directed several radio, theater, and television foundations. Initially linked to surrealism, Elytis was a prolific poet, his most celebrated book being *To Áxion Estí*, as well as an art critic and translator of major French, Italian, Russian, German, and Spanish authors. He received the 1979 Nobel Prize in Literature.

Robert Frost (1874–1963) was born in San Francisco and moved to New England at age eleven. Enrolled at Dartmouth and Harvard, he never earned a degree. Frost moved to England in 1912, returning to America three years later. His poetry volumes include *A Boy's Will*; *North of Boston*; *New Hampshire*, winner of the Pulitzer Prize; *West-Running Brook*; *Collected Poems*, also awarded the Pulitzer; *The Lovely Shall Be Choosers*; *A Further Range*, which earned Frost his third Pulitzer; *From Snow to Snow*; *A Witness Tree*, awarded another Pulitzer, making Frost the first person to win the prize four times; *Steeple Bush*; and *Hard Not to Be King*. He received the Bollingen Prize.

Gloria Fuertes (1918–1998) was born in Madrid. She began her literary career as an author of children's stories and poems and won several awards for her children's writing. An editor, librarian, and teacher, she received a Fulbright and spent three years teaching Spanish literature in the United States. Among her poetry books are *Isla ignorada*; *Pirulí*; *Todo asusta*; ...*Que estás en la tierra*, which brought her wider acclaim; *Ni tiro, ni veneno, ni navaja*, which garnered the Guipúzcoa prize; *Poeta de guardia*; and *Sola en la sala*.

Irwin Allen Ginsberg (1926–1997) was born in Newark, New Jersey. A major "Beat generation" writer linked to the San Francisco Renaissance, Ginsberg was also an active, outspoken political and social critic, especially regarding the Vietnam War, American materialist culture, and gay rights. A practicing Buddhist, he helped to found the Jack Kerouac School of Disembodied Poetics, at Trungpa's Naropa Institute. He traveled widely to Mexico, India, Japan, Cuba, and Czechosolvakia. His many books of poetry include *Howl and Other Poems*; *Kaddish and Other Poems*; *Reality Sandwiches*; *The Fall of America*, which won the National Book Award; and *White Shroud*.

Thom Gunn (1929–2004) was born in Gravesend, Kent, in England, and lived in San Francisco from 1954 until his death. His numerous volumes of poetry include *Fighting Terms*, *Moly*, *Jack Straw's Castle*, *The Passages of Joy*, *The Man with Night Sweats*, and *Boss Cupid*, and he published several collections of essays, most notably *The Occasions of Poetry*. Among his honors were the Lila Acheson Wallace/Reader's Digest fellowship, the Robert Kirsch Award from the *Los Angeles Times*, the Lenore Marshall/*Nation* Poetry Prize, and MacArthur and Guggenheim fellowships.

Born in Dorsetshire, England, and trained as an architect, **Thomas Hardy** (1840–1928) began his career as a novelist with *Desperate Remedies*. That book was followed by *Under the Greenwood Tree*, *Far from the Madding Crowd*, *The Return of the Native*, *The Mayor of Casterbridge*, *Tess of the D'Urbervilles*, *Jude the Obscure*, which caused a moral scandal, and others. He left fiction for poetry, and his eight verse collections are *Wessex Poems*, *Poems of the Past and Present*, *Time's Laughingstocks*, *Satires of Circumstance*, *Moments of Vision*, *Late Lyrics and Earlier*, *Human Shows*, and *Winter Words in Various Moods and Meters*. Hardy wrote a three-volume epic-drama about the Napoleonic wars, *The Dynasts*.

Gwen Harwood (1920–1995) was born in Brisbane in Queensland, Australia. Her many books include two volumes of *Poems*, along with *The Lion's Bride*, *Bone Scan*, and *The Present Tense*. She received the Grace Leven Prize, the Robert Frost Award, the Patrick White Award, the Victorian Premier's Literary Award, and the J.J. Bray Award, while *Blessed City*, her collected letters, was Age Book of the Year. Also a literary critic and librettist, Harwood lived mainly in Tasmania, receiving an honorary doctorate from the University of Tasmania in 1988.

Robert Hayden (1913–1980) was born as Bundy Sheffey in Detroit, Michigan. From 1936 to 1938 he worked for the Federal Writers' Project. His individual poetry books are *Heart-Shape in the Dust*, *A Ballad of Remembrance*—awarded the grand prize for poetry at the First World Festival of Negro Arts in Dakar, Senegal—*The Lion and the Archer*, *Figures of Time*, *Words in the Mourning Time*, *The Night-Blooming Cereus*, *Angle of Ascent*, and *American Journal*. In 1976 he became the first African American to be appointed Consultant in Poetry to the Library of Congress.

Anthony Hecht was born in New York City in 1923. He won the Pulitzer Prize for *The Hard Hours*, and his other books of poetry include *The Darkness and the Light*, *Flight Among the Tombs*, *The Transparent Man*, *The Venetian Vespers*, *Millions of Strange Shadows*, and *A Summoning of Stones*. He has authored three books of criticism and cotranslated Aeschylus. Hecht has received the Bollingen Prize, the Ruth Lilly Prize, the Eugenio Montale Award, and the Harriet Monroe Poetry Award, as well as fellowships from the Ford, Guggenheim, and Rockefeller Foundations.

Zbigniew Herbert (1924–1998) was born in Lwow, Poland. As a teen he fought in the underground resistance against the Nazis and studied law, economics, and philosophy. He wrote many volumes of poetry, among them *Pan Cogito* and *Raport z oblezonego miasta i inne wiersze*, along with several plays and books of essays. Herbert traveled extensively in France, England, Italy, and Greece, and his numerous international awards included the Jerusalem Literature Prize, the Herder Prize, the Nicholaus Lenau Prize, the Koscielski Prize, and an award from the Polish Institute of Arts and Sciences in America.

Born in Salonika, Turkish poet, playwright, and novelist **Nazim Hikmet** (1902–1963) was raised in Istanbul. After World War I he studied economics and social studies at the University of Moscow. In 1926, after Hikmet returned to Istanbul, the Ankara Independence Tribunal sentenced him to fifteen years of hard labor and exile for one of his poems. Thereafter, his life as an ardent Communist fluctuated among prison, short-lived amnesty, and constant flight. He was a prolific poet, his work moving from early patriotic hymns in regular meter to texts influenced by Russian futurism. He died in Moscow.

Max Jacob (1876–1944) was born in Quimper, in Brittany, France, and trained in painting at the Académie Julian. He associated with surrealism and the early twentieth-century Paris art scene. In 1921, after converting to Catholicism, the Jewish-born poet, painter, writer, and critic moved to the monastery of St. Benoît-sur-Loire. His most famous volume of poems is *Le Cornet à Dés*. Poor his entire life, Jacob worked odd jobs. He was arrested by the Nazis in 1944 and died of bronchial pneumonia in a concentration camp at Drancy, near Paris. He had become a Chevalier of the Légion d'honneur in 1933.

Francis Jammes (1868–1938) was born in Tournay in Hautes-Pyrénées, France. His principal works include *De l'Angélus de l'aube à l'Angélus du soir*, *Le deuil des primevères*, *Le triomphe de la vie*, *L'église habillée de feuilles*, *La Vierge et les Sonnets*, *Le Rosaire au soleil*, *Les Géorgiques chrétiennes*, *Le livre des quatrain*, *De tout temps à jamais*, *Lavigerie*, *Le Rêve franciscain*, and *Sources*. In 1917 he was awarded the Grand Prix of l'Académie Française. A convert to Catholicism and the father of seven children, Jammes died in Hasparren, in the Pyrénées-Atlantiques.

John Robinson Jeffers (1887–1962) was born in Pittsburgh, Pennsylvania. Educated in Switzerland and the United States, his diverse studies included Greek, Latin, and Old English, French literary history and the history of the Roman Empire, Dante, Spanish romantic poetry, philosophy and medicine, and forestry. Among his poetry books are *Californians*; *Roan Stallion, Tamar, and Other Poems*; *The Women at Point Sur*; *Cawdor and Other Poems*; *Thurso's Landing*; *Give Your Heart to the Hawks*; *Solstice and Other Poems*; *Be Angry at the Sun*; *The Double Axe and Other Poems*; and *Hungerfield and Other Poems*. His adaptation of Euripides's *Medea* was produced in New York.

Poet, essayist, translator, and critic **Roberto Juarroz** (1925–1995) was born in Coronel Dorrego, a province of Buenos Aires, Argentina. He studied at the University of Buenos Aires and at the Sorbonne, later acting as director of the former's Department of Bibliotecology and Documentation for thirty years. Juarroz received numerous international prizes for his writing, including the Grand Prize of Honor of the Fundación Argentina para la Poesía; the Esteban Echeverría prize, given annually by the Asociación Gente de Letras de Buenos Aires for lifetime achievement; the Jean Malrieu de Marsella prize; and the Bienal Internacional de Poesía prize.

Donald Justice (1925–2004) was born in Miami, Florida, and studied musical composition at university. His first poetry book, *The Summer Anniversaries*, was a Lamont Poetry Selection, and subsequent volumes include *Night Light*; *Departures*; *Selected Poems*, which won the Pulitzer Prize; and *New and Selected Poems*. He also published a collection of essays and interviews, *Platonic Scripts*, as well as a volume of poems, stories, and memoir, *The Sunset Maker*. Justice was awarded the Bollingen Prize and grants from the Guggenheim and Rockefeller Foundations.

Kenneth Koch (1925–2002) was born in Cincinnati, Ohio. He wrote nearly thirty books of poems, including *Ko, or A Season on Earth*; *Thank You and Other Poems*; *When the Sun Tries to Go On*; *The Art of Love*; *The Burning Mystery of Anna in 1951*; *Days and Nights*; *One Train*; and *New Addresses*. He also wrote fiction, drama, and books about teaching poetry, especially to children, such as *Rose, Where Did You Get That Red?* A finalist for the National Book Award, Koch won the Bollingen Prize and the Bobbitt Library of Congress Poetry Prize.

Philip Larkin (1922–1985) was born in Coventry, England. His four books of poetry are *The North Ship*, *The Less Deceived*, *The Whitsun Weddings*, and *High Windows*. An avatar of the neo-Romantic, formalist movement known as "The Movement," Larkin also authored two novels, *Jill* and *A Girl in Winter*, as well as criticism of literature and jazz, which appeared as *All What Jazz: A Record Diary 1961–68* and *Required Writing: Miscellaneous Pieces 1955–1982*. He died in Hull, where he had been a librarian.

David Herbert Lawrence (1885–1930) was born in Eastwood, Nottinghamshire, in England. His first published works were poems, and his volumes, generally published at intervals of a year or two, include *Love Poems and Others*; *Amores*; *Look! We Have Come Through*; *Bay*; *Tortoises*; *Birds, Beasts and Flowers*; *Pansies*, which was banned in England; and *Nettles*. Lawrence fought tuberculosis, censorship—most notably toward his novel *Lady Chatterly's Lover*, though *Sons and Lovers* and *Women in Love* were also scandalous—and, during World War I, accusations of his wife's pro-Germanism. He wrote non-fiction about pornography, democracy, psychoanalysis, and literature. He died in France, having traveled around the world.

Enrique Lihn (1929–1988) was born in Santiago, Chile. His first poetry volume, *Nada se escurre*, appeared when he was twenty. He traveled to Europe on a UNESCO fellowship to study museums and became chief editor of *Germán Marín Cormorán*, a monthly review of art, literature, and social science. In 1975 Lihn received an invitation from the French government and went there, writing *Paris, situación irregular*, while a Guggenheim took him to the United States, resulting in *A partir de Manhattan* and the later *Pena de extrañamiento*, his memories of that city. He also wrote a pair of novels, *La orquesta de crystal* and *El arte de la palabra*.

Jorge Mateus de Lima (1893–1953), born in União dos Palmares, Brazil, was a teacher, legislator, and physician. His books of poetry include *Poemas, Novos poemas, Tempo et eternidade, Poemas escolhidos, A túnica inconsútil, Poemas negros, As Ilhas*, and *Invenção de Orfeu*. A second-generation modernist, de Lima received the Graca Aranha Foundation literary award, the *Revista Americana* award, and the Grande Prêmio de Poesia from the Brazilian Academy of Letters. He died in Rio de Janeiro.

Federico García Lorca (1899–1936) was born in Fuente Vaqueros, Spain. He published his first book, *Impresiones y Viajes*, in 1919 and traveled to Madrid, where he wrote *Libro de poemas*, based on Spanish folklore, organized the first "Cante Jondo" festival of "deep song" singers and guitarists, and joined the "Generación del 27," which introduced him to surrealism. His other verse books include *Romancero Gitano, El poema del Cante Jondo, Llanto por Ignacio Sanchez Mejias*, and *Poeta en Nueva York*. In 1929 he visited New York City, returning to Spain after the proclamation of the Spanish republic. He was killed by Franquist soldiers at the outbreak of the Spanish Civil War. Among his plays are *La zapatera prodigiosa, Bodas de sangre, Yerma*, and *La Casa de Bernarda Alba*.

Robert Traill Spence Lowell (1917–1977) was born in Boston. His many books include *Land of Unlikeness*; *Lord Weary's Castle*, for which he was given the Pulitzer; *The Mills of the Kavanaughs*; National Book Award winner *Life Studies*; *Imitations*, his loose translations of Rilke, Rimbaud, and others that won the Bollingen Poetry Translation Prize; *For the Union Dead*; *Near the Ocean*; *Notebooks, 1967–1968*; *History*; *For Lizzy and Harriet*; *The Dolphin*, recipient of another Pulitzer; and *Day by Day*. A convert to Catholicism, Lowell was repeatedly hospitalized for manic depression and mental breakdown. He was a conscientious objector during World War II and opposed to the war in Vietnam.

James Merrill (1926–1995) was born in New York City. By the time he graduated from Amherst College, his poetry had already appeared in *Poetry* and *The Kenyon Review*, and he had published his first book, *The Black Swan*. He traveled through Europe and Asia, eventually residing between Connecticut, Florida, and Greece. He published novels, short stories, drama, and memoir but is best known for his poetry. Among his volumes are *Water Street*; *Nights and Days*, winner of the National Book Award; *The Fire Screen*; *Braving the Elements*, which led to the Bollingen Prize; *Divine Comedies*, which won the Pulitzer Prize; *The Changing Light at Sandover*; *The Inner Room*; and the posthumously published *A Scattering of Salts*.

William Stanley Merwin was born in New York City in 1927. His poetry books include *The Pupil*; *The River Sound*, which was named a *New York Times* Notable Book of the Year; *The Folding Cliffs*; *The Vixen*; *Travels*, which won the Lenore Marshall Poetry Prize; *The Rain in the Trees*; *The Carrier of Ladders*, which received the Pulitzer Prize; *The Lice*; and *A Mask for Janus*, which was selected for the Yale Series of Younger Poets. He has published numerous volumes of translation, plays, and prose. His honors include the Bollingen Prize, the Ruth Lilly Poetry Prize, the PEN Translation Prize, and a Lila Wallace-Reader's Digest Award, as well as fellowships from the Guggenheim, Rockefeller, and Ford Foundations.

Henri Michaux (1899–1984) was born in Namur, Belgium. He contemplated priesthood, turned instead to medicine, and then left school to enlist in the merchant marine. His travels through the Americas, Asia, Africa, India, and China inspired much of his work, including *Ecuador*, *Barbare en Asie*, and *Ailleurs*. He settled in Paris, where he became a painter. Among his many poetry volumes are *Qui je fus*; *La Nuit remue*; *Un Certain Plume*; and *Poteaux d'angle*. Michaux's *Nous Deux Encore* addresses his relation with his wife and the aftermath of her death in 1948, while *Misérable Miracle*, *L'infini Turbulent*, and *Paix dans les Brisements* document his experiments with mescaline. In 1965 he refused the Grand Prix National des Lettres. Michaux died in Paris, having become a French citizen in 1950.

Edna St. Vincent Millay (1892–1950) was born in Rockland, Maine. At age twenty she won fourth place in a contest for her poem "Renascence," and its publication in *The Lyric Year* earned her a scholarship to Vassar. Upon graduating, Millay published her first book, *Renascence and Other Poems*, and relocated to Greenwich Village. Thereafter she lived in Paris, Rome, Vienna, and Budapest, eventually settling in the Berkshires. Her volume *A Few Figs from Thistles* was controversial for its depictions of female sexuality and feminist ideals, while *The Harp Weaver* was awarded the Pulitzer Prize. She published another dozen poetry books, also writing plays and the libretto for *The King's Henchman*.

Czesław Miłosz (1911–2004) was born in Szetejnie, Lithuania, then under Russian control. Cofounder of the avant-garde literary group Zagary, he worked for Polish radio and for underground Warsaw presses during World War II, afterward traveling to Washington and New York as a Polish diplomat, then to Paris where he received political asylum, and eventually settled in Berkeley. In addition to numerous poetry volumes, he translated Baudelaire, Eliot, Milton, Shakespeare, Whitman, and the Bible. Miłosz's *Zniewolony Umysl*, which examined the complexities of intellectuals living under Stalinism, received the Prix Littéraire European. His other honors included the Nobel Prize for Literature and the Neustadt International Prize.

Eugenio Montale (1896–1981) was born in Genoa, Italy, and trained to be an opera singer. He was dismissed from his directorship of the Gabinetto Vieusseux research library for refusing to join the Fascist party. His poetry books include *Ossi di sepia, Le occasioni, La bufera e altro, Satura, Diario del '71 e del '72, Quaderno di quattro anni*, and *Altri versi e poesi disperse*. The author of essays, short stories, travel sketches, and music criticism, as well as a painter and literary critic for *Corriere della Sera*, Montale also translated Shakespeare, Melville, O'Neill, and T. S. Eliot. He was named a lifetime member of the Italian Senate in 1967 and received the Nobel Prize for Literature in 1975.

Marianne Craig Moore (1887–1972) was born in Kirkwood, Missouri. After a stint as a schoolteacher, she became an assistant at the New York Public Library. She served as acting editor of the *Dial* from 1925 to 1929 and translated La Fontaine's *Fables choisies*. H.D. published Moore's first book of poetry, *Poems*, without her knowledge in 1921. Her other individual volumes are *Observations, The Pangolin and Other Verse, What Are Years?, Nevertheless, Like a Bulwark, O to Be a Dragon, The Arctic Fox*, and *Tell Me, Tell Me*. Her *Collected Poems* won the Pulitzer Prize, the National Book Award, and the Bollingen Prize.

Moore's other achievements included the Helen Haire Levinson Prize and a Guggenheim fellowship.

Edwin Muir (1887–1959) hailed from Deerness, in the Orkney Islands of Scotland, and moved to Glasgow at age fourteen. He published three novels, a controversial assessment of Scottish culture titled *Scott and Scotland*, several volumes of literary and social criticism, the memoir *An Autobiography*, and the poetry collections *First Poems, Variations on a Time Theme, Journeys and Places, The Narrow Place, The Voyage, The Labyrinth*, and *One Foot in Eden*. Muir and his wife Willa (*née* Anderson) lived in London, Sussex, St. Andrews, Edinburgh, Prague, Rome, Vienna, and elsewhere, and cotranslated Franz Kafka and Hermann Broch.

Frederick Ogden Nash (1902–1971) was born in Rye, New York, and raised in Savannah, Georgia. First a teacher, then a salesman, Nash was writing advertising copy for Doubleday/Page Publishing in New York when his first children's book, *The Cricket of Caradon*, appeared in 1925. Nash's first poem was published five years later, in *The New Yorker*, whose staff he eventually joined. He authored nineteen volumes of poetry, including *Hard Lines* and *I'm a Stranger Here Myself*, as well as many books for kids, and also collaborated on the Broadway musical comedy *One Touch of Venus*. He died at home in Baltimore.

Pablo Neruda (1904–1973) was born Neftalí Ricardo Reyes Basoalto in Parral, Chile. He published his first volume, *Crepusculario*, at age nineteen, using a pseudonym because his family disapproved of his occupation. After *Veinte poemas de amor y una cancion desesperada*, he quit school to devote himself to poetry. His volumes include *Residencia en la tierra, Las Uvas y el Viento, Odas elementales, Cien sonetos de amor, Las manos del día, Fin del mundo*, and *Las piedras del cielo*. Neruda was sympathetic to the loyalists during the Spanish Civil War, when he wrote *España en el Corazón*, later publishing *Canto General de Chile* during his exile from his native country when Communism was declared illegal. A career diplomat, Neruda served in Burma, Ceylon, Argentina, Spain, Mexico, and France, and was elected senator of the Republic in 1945. He received the 1971 Nobel Prize for Literature.

Francis Russell O'Hara (1926–1966) was born in Baltimore, Maryland, and studied piano at the New England Conservatory. He served in the South Pacific and Japan during World War II, before attending Harvard and Michigan, working as an employee of the Museum of Modern Art in New York City, and writing essays on painting and sculpture for *ArtNews*. A founding member of the New York School of poets and painters, O'Hara sometimes collaborated with artists to make "poem-paintings" and also wrote drama. His six volumes of poetry are *A City in Winter, Meditations in* *an Emergency, Odes, Second Avenue, Lunch Poems*, and *In Memory of My Feelings*.

George Oppen (1908–1984) was born in New Rochelle, New York. He was declared an objectivist poet and, while initially rejecting the presence of any such movement, assisted in the creation of the Objectivist Press. He became a Communist in the 1930s, working with the unemployed in New York City, lobbying for social services, and organizing industrial workers in Utica, New York. He saw six months of action in World War II. Oppen's books are *Discrete Series*; *The Materials*; *This in Which*; *Of Being Numerous*, which won the Pulitzer Prize; and *Primitive*. His collected poetry was nominated for a National Book Award.

Wilfred Edward Salter Owen (1893–1918) was born in Oswestry, England. A teacher of English in France, he decided in 1915 to return home and enlist in the Artists's Rifles. He wrote most of his important war poetry while convalescing at Craiglockhart War Hospital near Edinburgh. Sent back into action, Owen, a second lieutenant, was killed on the French front in a German machine gun attack, his war experience having totaled four months. English composer Benjamin Britten later used several of Owen's poems and fragments in his *War Requiem*.

Dan Pagis (1930–1986) was born in Bukovina, Romania. Interned in a concentration camp during World War II, he settled in Israel in 1946, started writing in Hebrew four years later, became a schoolteacher on a kibbutz and eventually a professor of medieval Hebrew literature at Hebrew University. He also taught at the Jewish Theological Seminary in New York, Harvard, the University of California at San Diego, and Berkeley. His poetry volumes include *Shaon Ha-Hol, Sheut Meuheret, Gilgul, Moah, Milim Nirdafot, Shneim Asar Panim*, and *Shirim Aharonim*.

Nicanor Parra was born in 1914 in San Fabián de Alico, Chile. He studied mathematics and theoretical physics and has taught in Chile, the United States, and England. His poetry books include *Cancionero sin Nombre, Poemas y Antipoemas, Versos de Salon, Canciones Rusas, Ejercicios Respiratorios*, and *Obra gruesa*, which won the Premio Nacional de Literatura. He has also won the Premio Internacional Juan Rulfo, the Prometeo de Poesía prize, the Premio Municipal de Poesía de Santiago, the Premio de Poesía Juan Said de la Sociedad de Escritores de Chile, the Premio Sindicato de Escritores de Chile, and the Luis Oyarzún prize. He coauthored *Discursos* with Pablo Neruda.

Boris Leonidovich Pasternak (1890–1960) was born in Moscow. He studied musical composition for six years, giving it up in 1909 to pursue law at

Moscow University. He then studied philosophy, which he in turn abandoned for poetry. Popular in the wake of the Russian Revolution of 1917, Pasternak fell out of favor with the Soviets in the 1930s. His major poetry volumes include *Sestra moya zhizn, Temy i variatsii, Vysokaya bolezn, Detstvo Lyuvers, Leytenant Shmidt, Devyatsot pyaty god, Vtoroye rozhdenie,* and *Na rannikh poyezdakh.* He also wrote autobiography, short fiction, and novels—most notably *Doktor Zhivago*—as well as translating plays by Shakespeare, Kleist, and Ben Jonson and poems by Hans Sachs, Goethe, and Harwegh. Pasternak was awarded the Nobel Prize in Literature in 1958.

Cesare Pavese (1908–1950) was born in Piedmont, Italy, and graduated from the University of Turin with a thesis on Whitman. He translated numerous authors from English, including Melville, Joyce, Stein, Hemingway, Faulkner, Dickens, Dos Passos, and Defoe. He was briefly exiled by the Fascists in 1935, before returning to Turin, where he edited *La Cultura* and directed the publisher Giulio Einaudi Editore. His first book of poems, *Lavorara stanca,* was published in 1936. His novels include *Il carcere, Tra Donne Sole,* and *La luna e i falò,* which won the Premio Strega. Among his posthumous publications are diaries, letters, further novels, and a second poetry collection, *Verrà la morte e avrà i tuoi occhi.*

Octavio Paz (1914–1998) was born in Mexico City. As a youth, under the sway of surrealism, he founded an avant-garde literary journal, *Barandal,* before publishing his first book of poems, *Luna Silvestre.* Further books include *Aguila o sol?, Piedra de Sol, Salamandra, Pasado en claro,* and *Vuelta.* In 1937 he traveled to Spain, to participate in the Second International Congress of Anti-Fascist Writers. Paz authored several volumes of social, political, and cultural commentary, among them *El laberinto de la soledad,* a study of Mexican identity; *Posdata; Los hijos del limo;* and *La otra voz.* He received the Cervantes award, the American Neustadt Prize, and the 1990 Nobel Prize for Literature.

Fernando Pessoa (1888–1935) was born Fernando António Nogueira Pêssoa in Lisbon, Portugal, and attended an English school in Durban, South Africa. After dropping out of university, he made his living by translating, writing criticism, and drafting business letters. He began publishing poetry in 1914, adopting the heteronyms Alberto Caeiro, Ricardo Reis, and Álvaro de Campos, each bearing a distinct personality, aesthetic, politics, and literary style. Pessoa published three books of poems in English—*Antinous, Sonnets,* and *English Poems*—but only one poetry book in Portuguese, *Mensagem,* appeared during his lifetime. Pessoa invented numerous other alter egos, among them Bernardo Soares, who authored *O Livro do Desassossego.*

Born in Montpellier, France, **Francis Ponge** (1899–1988) studied law in Paris and literature in Strasbourg. An editor and journalist, he became attached to *La Nouvelle Revue Française*, then to surrealism and communism. He lived in Algeria for two years before working as a professor at the Alliance Française in Paris for over a decade. His works, many of them prose poetry, include *Le Parti-pris des choses*, *Le Savon*, *La Pratique de la littérature*, *Pièces*, *Pour un Malherbe*, and *La Rage de l'expression*. He was awarded the Books Abroad/Neustadt International Prize for Literature in 1974.

Vasko Popa (1922–1991) was born in Grebenac, Banat, in Yugoslavia. He studied French and Yugoslav literature at the universities of Vienna, Bucharest, and Belgrade, later working as an editor at the Nolit publishing house in Belgrade. He was the author of eight volumes of poetry, including *Kora*, *Nepočin-Polje*, *Pesme*, and *Sporedno Nebo*. Popa received a number of literary awards: the Branko Radičevič prize, the Zmaj prize, the Lenau prize, the National Austrian Prize for European Literature, the Seventh of July prize, and many others.

Ezra Pound (1885–1972) was born in Hailey, Idaho. In 1917 he became the London editor of the *Little Review*, later moving to Italy. He did not return to the United States until 1945, when he was arrested on charges of treason for having broadcast Fascist propaganda over radio to the United States during World War II. Acquitted, he was declared mentally ill and committed to St. Elizabeth's Hospital in Washington, D.C. His poetry volumes include *Personae*, *Lustra and Other Poems*, *Umbra*, *Homage to Sextus Propertius*, *The Pisan Cantos*, which received the Bollingen Prize and hence caused a controversy, and *The Cantos*. Pound also translated widely and wrote many critical books, such as *Make It New*, *The ABC of Reading*, and *Guide to Kulchur*.

Jacques Prévert (1907–1977) was born in Neuilly-sur-Seine, France. An ardent surrealist early on, he wrote children's books, comic books, ballets, libretti, popular songs, and plays that he sometimes acted in. Among his poetry books are *Paroles*, *Histoires*, *Spectacle*, *La Pluie et beau temps*, and *Choses et autres*. In addition, Prévert created collages and wrote screenplays, most notably for director Marcel Carné, including *Les enfants du paradis*, *Drôle de drame*, *Les Portes de la nuit*, and *Le jour se lève*.

Born in Le Havre, **Raymond Queneau** (1903–1976) went to Paris at age seventeen and was briefly in Breton's surrealist group. His first novel, *Le Chiendent*, was followed by *Les enfants du limon*, *Odile*, *Loin de Rueil*, *Le Dimanche de la vie*, *Zazie dans le metro*, which was filmed by Louis Malle,

Les fleurs bleues, and others, while *Petite Cosmogonie Portative, Cent Mille Milliards de Poèmes,* and *Exercices de style* subvert genre classification. In 1950, Queneau joined the Collège of Pataphysique, which investigated eccentric exceptions to natural laws, and a decade later he cofounded "Oulipo," or Ouvroir de Littérature Potentielle. Director of the *Encyclopédie de la Pléiade,* Queneau also wrote essays, including *Bâtons, chiffres et letters* and *Bordes.*

Rainer Maria Rilke (1875–1926) was born in Prague. His first trio of poetry books—*Leben und Lieder, Larenopfer,* and *Traumgekrönt*—was published by 1896, when he left Charles University to travel to Germany, Italy, and Russia. In 1902, during a twelve-year residence in Paris, he became the friend and secretary of Rodin. With the onset of World War I, Rilke relocated to Munich, before settling in Switzerland, where he lived the rest of his life. His major volumes of poetry and prose include *Das Stunden Buch, Neue Gedichte, Requiem, Das Marienleben, Die Sonette an Orpheus, Duineser Elegen, Das Buch vom lieben Gott und anderes,* and *Die Aufzeichnungen des Malte Laurids Brigge.*

Yannos Ritsos (1909–1990) was born in Monembasia, Greece. As a young man he spent four years in a sanatorium to cure his tuberculosis. He was aligned with communism and futurism, and his first book, *Trakter,* hailed a new moment in Greek poetry. It was followed by *Epitaphios,* which was burned publicly by a dictatorial regime, *To Tragoudi Tis Adelfis Mou, Dokimasia, To Dentro Tis Fylakis Kai I Gynaikes,* and dozens of others. During the Greek civil war, the antifascist Ritsos spent four years in "rehabilitation" camps, and in 1967 another military junta deported him to Samos. He wrote many novels and received many international prizes. He died in Athens.

Theodore Huebner Roethke (1908–1963) was born in Saginaw, Michigan. His first book, *Open House,* took a decade to write and was followed by, among others, *The Lost Son; Praise to the End!; The Waking,* which won the Pulitzer Prize; and *Words for the Wind,* which received the Bollingen Prize, National Book Award, Edna St. Vincent Millay Prize, Longview Foundation Award, and the Pacific Northwest Writers Award. The posthumously published *The Far Field* won the National Book Award. Roethke earned a Guggenheim fellowship, *Poetry's* Levinson Prize, and grants from the Ford Foundation and the National Institute of Arts and Letters.

Polish poet, essayist, and playwright **Tadeusz Rozewicz** (born October 9, 1921, in Radomsk, Poland) is one of the great witnesses to the twentieth century. A fighter in the Polish resistance (1943–1944), Rozewicz gave voice to the crisis of values that the Holocaust wrought in the sharpest, most disturbing, and clear way, resulting in a new kind of poetic language: simple, minimalist, powerful and raw. No postwar Polish poet's influence on poetics has been felt more strongly than Rozewicz's. His plays *Card File* (1960) and *White Marriage* (1975) established him as a leading playwright. The decade comprising the years 1992–2002 saw an explosion of creativity, during which he published five collections of some of his best poetry, including *Recycling* (1996), *Mother Departs* (1999), and *The Professor's Knife* (2001).

Greek writer **George Seferis** (1900–1971) was born Giorgos Seferiadis in Smyrna, Turkey. He moved to Paris to study law, returning in 1925 to Athens, where he was admitted to the Royal Greek Ministry of Foreign Affairs. His long diplomatic career included posts in England, Albania, Turkey, Lebanon, Syria, Jordan, and Iraq. Among his poetry volumes are *Strophe, E Sterna, Mythistorema, Tetradio Gymnasmaton*, the *Emerologio Katastromatos* triptych, and *Tria Krypha Poiemata*. He published several books of essays and translations, including *Dokimes* and *Antigrafes*. He was awarded the Nobel Prize in Literature in 1963.

William De Witt Snodgrass was born in Wilkinsburg, Pennsylvania, in 1926. He has published over twenty books of poetry, most notably *Heart's Needle*, which won the Pulitzer Prize, and *The Führer Bunker*, nominated for the National Book Critics Circle Award. He has also written criticism, *To Sound Like Yourself: Essays on Poetry* and *In Radical Pursuit*, as well as six volumes of translation, of which *Selected Translations* won the Harold Morton Landon Translation Award. Among Snodgrass's other honors are the Guinness Poetry Award, Miles Modern Poetry Award, and fellowships from the Ford, Guggenheim, and Ingram Merrill Foundations.

Wallace Stevens (1879–1955) was born in Reading, Pennsylvania. Trained as a lawyer, he worked at the Hartford Accident and Indemnity Company in Connecticut, becoming its vice president in 1934. His major poetry volumes are *Harmonium*—published in 1923, when Stevens was forty-four—*Ideas of Order, The Man with the Blue Guitar, Parts of a World, Transport to Summer*, and *The Auroras of Autumn*, which won the National Book Award. Winner of the Bollingen Prize, Stevens received the Pulitzer Prize and another National Book Award for his *Collected Poems*. He also published *The Necessary Angel: Essays on Reality and the Imagination*.

Ruth Stone was born in 1915 in Roanoke, Virginia. Her poetry books include *In the Next Galaxy*, winner of the National Book Award; *Ordinary Words*, which received the National Book Critics Circle Award; *Simplicity*; *Who is the Widow's Muse?*; *Second-Hand Coat*; *Cheap*; *Topography and*

Other Poems; and *In an Iridescent Time*. She has been the recipient of the Bunting Fellowship, the Delmore Schwartz Award, the Wallace Stevens Award, a Whiting Writers Award, two Guggenheim fellowships, the Bess Hokin Award, the *Kenyon Review* Fellowship in Poetry, the Shelley Memorial Award, and the Vermont Cerf Award.

Jules Supervielle (1884–1960) was born in Montevideo, Uruguay, and educated in Paris. His poetry volumes include *Débarcadères*, *Gravitations*, *Le Forçat innocent*, *Amis inconnus*, *La Fable du monde*, *Oublieuse mémoire*, *A la nuit*, *Naissances*, *L'Escalier*, and *Le Corps tragique*. His conception of poetry is outlined in *En songeant à un art poétique*, while *Boire à la source* is an autobiographical récit. Supervielle also authored novels, including *L'Homme de la pampa* and *Le Survivant*, several short story collections, four plays, and many translations. He died in Paris, having divided his life between France and Uruguay.

May Swenson (1919–1989) was born in Logan, Utah. An editor at New Directions from 1959 to 1966, she also taught poetry at a number of American universities. Her poetry volumes are *Another Animal*; *A Cage of Spines*; *To Mix with Time: New and Selected Poems*; *Half Sun, Half Sleep*; *New and Selected Things Taking Place*; and *In Other Words*. She also authored a volume of prose, *The Contemporary Poet as Artist and Critic*; two books of children's verse, *Poems to Solve* and *More Poems to Solve*; and translations of Tranströmer and other Swedish poets.

Wisława Szymborska was born in Bnin, Poland, in 1923. She has published more than fifteen poetry volumes, including *Chwila*, *Widok z ziarnkiem piasku*, *102 wiersze*, *Ludzie na moscie*, *Poezje wybrane* and *Poezje wybrane II*, *Wybór wierszy*, and *Wolanie do Yeti*. Her early work, such as *Dlatego zyjemy*, was inflected by social realism. A book reviewer and translator of French poetry, she served on the editorial staff of *Zycie Literackie* from 1953 to 1981, while in the 1980s she wrote for the underground press under the pseudonym Stancykówna and for a magazine in Paris. Winner of the Nobel Prize for Literature in 1996, Szymborska has also received the Goethe Prize, the Herder Prize, and the prize of the Polish PEN Club.

Dylan Marlais Thomas (1914–1953) was born in Swansea, Wales, and dropped out of school at age sixteen. His first book, *Eighteen Poems*, appeared when he was twenty, to great success; and his others are *Twenty-Five Poems*, *The World I Breath*, *The Map of Love*, *New Poems*, *Deaths and Entrances*, and *In Country Sleep and Other Poems*. He authored one play, *Under Milkwood*, and several volumes of prose, such as *The Portrait of the Artist as a Young Dog*, *A Child's Christmas in Wales*, and the unfinished

Adventures in the Skin Trade. Thomas visited the United States in 1950, on a reading tour, and later died in New York City.

Welsh writer **Edward Philip Thomas** (1878–1917) was born in London and educated at Oxford, where he studied history. He began writing poems in 1914, after a visit from Robert Frost. In his first volume, *Six Poems*, he adopted the pseudonym Edward Eastaway, to separate his poetry from his professional journalism, editing, and writing on local history. He authored a life of Richard Jefferies; studies of Swinburne, Keats, and Pater; the novel *The Happy-Go-Lucky Morgans*; and numerous accounts of rural life, such as *The Heart of England, The South Country*, and *The Icknield Way*. He joined the Artists' Rifles in 1915, was commissioned a second lieutenant, and volunteered for overseas duty. He was killed at Ronville.

Tomas Tranströmer was born in Stockholm, Sweden, in 1931. A psychologist, he has worked at Roxtuna Prison for Boys and with the occupationally handicapped, providing vocational guidance and assisting rehabilitation. Among his poetry volumes are *17 dikter; Hemligheter på vägen; Den halvfärdiga himlen; Klanger och spar; Mörkerseende; Stigar; Östersjöar; Sanningsbarriären; Det vilda torget; För levande och döda;* and *Sorgegondolen*. His many honors include the Bonnier Award for Poetry, the German Petrarch Prize, and the Neustadt International Prize for Literature. His work has been translated into nearly fifty languages.

Marina Tsvetaeva (1892–1941) was born in Moscow. Her first poetry book, *Vechernii al'bom*, was published when she was eighteen and received favorably. After the Russian Revolution, which she opposed, she lived in Prague, Berlin, and Paris. Upon returning to Russia, her husband was shot. At the outbreak of World War II, Tsvetaeva fled to Yelabuga, where she hanged herself. The author of plays and criticism, her other poetry volumes include *Volshebnyi fonar', Versty* and *Versty II, Stikhi k Bloku, Razluka, Remeslo, Psikheya*, and *Posle Rossii*.

Xavier Villaurrutia (1903–1950) was born in Mexico City. He graduated from the National School of Jurisprudence, worked on the literary review *Contemporáneos*, and codirected the journal *Ulises*. He received a Rockefeller Foundation grant to study at the Yale School of Drama and founded the first experimental theater in Mexico, Teatro Ulises, in 1928. Villaurrutia's poetry volumes include *Reflejos, Nocturnos, Nostalgia de la muerte*, and *Décima muerte*. The author of several plays and short dramatic pieces, such as *Invitación a la muerte* and *Autos profanes*, he also translated major European dramatists.

Derek Walcott was born in Saint Lucia, the West Indies, in 1930. His poetry volumes include *Tiepolo's Hound, The Bounty, Omeros, The Arkansas Testament, Midsummer, The Fortunate Traveller, The Star-Apple Kingdom, Sea Grapes, Another Life, The Gulf, The Castaway*, and *In a Green Night*. Founder of the Trinidad Theater Workshop, Walcott is the author of numerous plays that have been produced throughout the United States, including *Dream on Monkey Mountain*, winner of the Obie Award. He is also an essayist and watercolor painter. Along with a MacArthur Foundation fellowship, a Royal Society of Literature Award, and the Queen's Medal for Poetry, he received the Nobel Prize in Literature in 1992.

Robert Penn Warren (1905–1989) was born in Guthrie, Kentucky. A "Fugitive" writer, he studied at Vanderbilt and, as a Rhodes scholar, at Oxford. He cofounded *The Southern Review* and cowrote the textbook *Understanding Poetry*. His poetry volumes include *Promises: Poems, 1954–1956*, which won the Sidney Hillman Award, the Edna St. Vincent Millay Memorial Award, the National Book Award, and the Pulitzer Prize; and *Now and Then: Poems, 1976–1978*, which won the Pulitzer. He was appointed the first U.S. Poet Laureate in 1985. Warren also wrote literary criticism; cultural commentary, such as the controversial *Who Speaks for the Negro?*; and children's books. Author of ten novels, he received the Pulitzer Prize for *All the King's Men*.

Richard Wilbur was born in New York City in 1921. His books of poetry include *New and Collected Poems*, which won the Pulitzer Prize; *The Mind-Reader; Walking to Sleep: New Poems and Translations; Advice to a Prophet and Other Poems; Things of This World*, a Pulitzer Prize and National Book Award winner; *Ceremony and Other Poems*; and *The Beautiful Changes and Other Poems*. He has also published translations of French drama, children's books, and collections of prose. A former U.S. Poet Laureate and a chevalier of the Ordre des Palmes Académiques, Wilbur has received the Bollingen Prize, the T.S. Eliot Award, a Ford Foundation Award, two Guggenheim fellowships, the Edna St. Vincent Millay Memorial Award, the Harriet Monroe Poetry Award, two PEN translation awards, and the Prix de Rome Fellowship.

William Carlos Williams (1883–1963) was born in Rutherford, New Jersey, and earned his M.D. from the University of Pennsylvania. His poetry volumes include *Poems; The Tempers; Al Que Quiere!; Kora in Hell: Improvisations; Spring and All; An Early Martyr; Broken Span; The Wedge; Clouds, Aigeltinger, Russia, &c.; The Desert Music and Other Poems; Pictures from Brueghel*; and the book-length epic *Paterson*. He also wrote novels, plays, and essays, among which are *White Mule, The Great American Novel, In the American Grain, Life along the Passaic River, Autobiography*, and *Imaginations*. He won the Bollingen and Pulitzer Prizes and the National Book Award.

James Arlington Wright (1927–1980) was born in Martins Ferry, Ohio. During World War II he was stationed in Japan during the American occupation; then he attended Kenyon College, the University of Vienna on a Fulbright, and the University of Washington, where he earned a Ph.D. on Dickens. Among his poetry books are *The Green Wall, Saint Judas, The Branch Will Not Break, Shall We Gather at the River, Two Citizens, Moments of the Italian Summer, To a Blossoming Pear Tree*, and *This Journey*. His *Collected Poems* received the Pulitzer Prize and earned him a Rockefeller Foundation grant.

Richard Wright (1908–1960) was born on a Mississippi plantation. He moved to Chicago in 1927, joined the Federal Writers' Project and the Communist Party, but later left the latter disillusioned. Between 1934 and 1941 he published more than a dozen poems in leftist journals such as *Partisan Review* and *New Masses*. After World War II he moved to Paris. Wright began writing haiku in the late 1950s and authored more than 4,000 during the last three years of his life. His novels include *Uncle Tom's Children* and *Native Son*, while *Black Boy* and the two-part *American Hunger* are autobiographical. *Twelve Million Black Voices* is his folk history of African America.

William Butler Yeats (1865–1939) was born in Dublin, Ireland. Involved with the Celtic Revival, Yeats was interested in theosophy, hermeticism, and the occult and engaged heavily in Irish politics, being appointed a senator of the Irish Free State in 1922. He authored many plays, Irish legends, and folkloric and fairy tales for children. His poetry books include *The Wanderings of Oisin and Other Poems*; *The Wind Among the Reeds*; *In the Seven Woods*; *The Green Helmet and Other Poems*; *Responsibilities*; *The Wild Swans at Coole*; *Michael Robartes and the Dancer*; *A Vision*; *The Tower*; *The Winding Stair*; and *New Poems*. He was awarded the Nobel Prize in Literature in 1923.

Andrea Zanzotto was born in 1921 in Pieve di Soligo, in Treviso, Italy. His poetry volumes include *Dietro il paesaggio*; *Elegia e altri versi*; *Vocativo*; *IX Ecloghe*; *La Beltà*; *Gli sguardi i fatti e senhal*; *Pasque*; *Il Galateo in Bosco*; *Fosfeni*; *Idioma*; *Meteo*; and *Sovrimpressioni*. The poem *Filò*, in original Veneto dialect, grew out of his collaboration with Federico Fellini on the film *Casanova*. Zanzotto is also the author of critical prose, including

Sull'Altopiano. He has won numerous awards, including the Premio Viareggio, Premio Librex-Montale, and the Premio "Feltrinelli" dell' Accademia dei Lincei.

A native of New York City, **Louis Zukofsky** (1904–1978) was the son of Orthodox Jews from Russia. By eleven he had read all of Shakespeare. He edited the "'Objectivists' 1931" issue of *Poetry*, followed by *An "Objectivists" Anthology*. Best known for his long poem *"A,"* begun in 1927, his shorter poems are collected in volumes such as *Anew, Some Time, Barely and Widely, I's (pronounced eyes)* and its sequel *After I's*, and *80 Flowers*. Zukofsky's prose works include short fiction, the two-volume *Bottom: On Shakespeare*, the teaching anthology *A Test of Poetry*, and *Le Style Apollinaire*.

INDEX